Science
ages 5-7

Suzanne Kirk

Published by Scholastic Ltd,
Villiers House,
Clarendon Avenue,
Leamington Spa,
Warwickshire
CV32 5PR
Text © Suzanne Kirk
© 2001
Scholastic Ltd
2 3 4 5 6 7 8 9 0   3 4 5 6 7 8 9 0

Author

Suzanne Kirk

Editor

Joel Lane

Assistant Editor

Alison Rosier

Series designer

Lynne Joesbury

Designers

David Hurley and Paul Cheshire

Illustrations

Lynda Murray

Cover illustration

Jill Newton

British Library Cataloguing-in-Publication Data
A catalogue record for this book is available from
the British Library.

ISBN 0-439-01786-6

ontents

Acknowledgements

Richard Edwards for the use of 'Ten Tall Oak Trees' from *Earthways Earthwise* edited by Judith Nicholls © 1993, Richard Edwards (1993, OUP).

Egmont Children's Books for the use of *Flat Stanley* by Jeff Brown © 1964, Jeff Brown (1964, Methuen Children's Books and Mammoth, imprints of Egmont Children's Books Limited, London).

Egmont Children's Books for the use of *The Owl Who Was Afraid of the Dark* by Jill Tomlinson © 1968, The Estate of Jill Tomlinson (1968, Methuen Children's Books and Mammoth, imprints of Egmont).

Jean Kenward for the use of 'Stones' by Jean Kenward from *Earthways Earthwise* edited by Judith Nicholls © 1993, Jean Kenward (1993, OUP).

Jean Kenward for the use of 'Dandelions' by Jean Kenward from *Earthways Earthwise* edited by Judith Nicholls © 1993, Jean Kenward (1993, OUP).

Larousse PLC for the use of 'The Giant Panda' by Philip Steele from the book *The Giant Panda* by Philip Steele © 1994, Grisewood & Dempsey (1994, Kingfisher).

The Lutterworth Press for the use of the material from *Whatever Happened in Winklesea* by Helen Cresswell © 1989, Helen Cresswell (1989, The Lutterworth Press).

Wes Magee for the use of 'Noisy (and Quiet) Places' from *Noisy Noise Annoys* by Wes Magee © 1996, Wes Magee (1996, Bodley Head).

Sarah Matthews for the use of 'Silverfish, Spiders and Flies' by Stanley Cook from *Come Along* by Stanley Cook © 1987 The Estate of Stanley Cook (1987, Blackie).

Sarah Matthews for the use of 'The Windmill' by Stanley Cook from *Another First Poetry Book* © 1992, The Estate of Stanley Cook (1992, OUP).

Eunice McMullen Literary Agent for the use of extracts from from the book *Dear Greenpeace* by Simon James © 1991, Simon James (1991, Walker Books).

The Peters, Fraser & Dunlop Group for the use of 'The Snowman' by Roger McGough from *Sky In The Pie* © 1983 Roger McGough (1983, Kestrel Books).

Marian Reiner Literary Agent for the use of 'Trees' by Harry Behn from *The Little Hill* by Harry Behn © 1949, renewed 1977 by Alice L. Behn, Harry Behn (1949).

Scholastic Children's Books for the use of *Dare You Make Friends With An Ugly Slug?* by Nick Arnold © 1996, Nick Arnold (1996, Scholastic Children's Books).

Ian Souter for the use of 'Surrounded by Noise' from *Earthways Earthwise* edited by Judith Nicholls © 1993, Ian Souter (1993, OUP).

Transworld Publishers for the use of 'Jolly Blue Giant' from the book *Jungle Jingles* by Dick King-Smith © 1990, Fox Busters (1990, published by Doubleday, a division of Transworld).

The Watts Publishing Group Ltd for the use of an extract 'How you can help your doctor' from *A Day In The Life of a Doctor* by Carol Watson © 1995, Franklin Watts (1995, Franklin Watts, a division of The Watts Publishing Group Ltd).

White Post Modern Farm Centre for the use of extracts from their brochure.

WWF-UK for the use of 'Brendan And The Whale' from the book *Our World, Our Water* by Ken Webster © 1996, WWF-UK (1996, WWF-UK).

Every effort has been made to trace copyright holders and the publishers apologize for any omissions.

Introduction

The texts that make up this book have been chosen to stimulate children's interest in both science and literature. They have been selected to be varied and informative, as well as enjoyable.

We cannot get away from science. It is always a part of our lives: it is both familiar and exotic. Children will learn that when we move about, look after ourselves, perform daily tasks and interact with the plants and animals that share our environment, we are experiencing science. Every day, we are dependent on scientific phenomena: we follow a pattern through our lives determined by the laws of science, and our present lifestyle is influenced by the achievements of great scientists. The future will be affected by the scientific knowledge and skills developed by the children of today.

A text with an appropriate scientific theme can be used to encourage a child's natural interest in things all around. It can provide opportunities for children to ask wide-ranging questions, give opinions and extend their thinking. It can help them to develop positive attitudes towards science, and in particular towards the environment. The content of such a text can lead them to develop the scientific skills of observing, exploring, recording and communicating.

Some texts deal with a single, narrow theme; but most can be used to make connections with several scientific ideas across the science curriculum. This is useful in developing children's awareness of a wider scientific picture – for example, linking 'senses' to 'growing up' or 'sharing the environment' to 'plant and animal life'.

Using these texts, children can enjoy the rhythm and rhyme of poetry and the emotions engendered by narrative. They can use their imagination to become involved in difficult or exciting situations. Presented with new information, they are encouraged to use it in widening their experience: to plant, collect, observe, sort and investigate.

Teaching science through texts

The texts can be used in different ways, depending on the science scheme of work, the time of year, topical issues and the children's interests:

◆ To introduce an area of science, when there are opportunities to assess the children's prior knowledge and review their understanding of key aspects.

◆ To use during the course of a unit of science, complementing the scheme of work and making links with other science topics.

◆ To extend children's particular area of interest, while consolidating or completing a unit of science work.

◆ To link with another text that deals with a similar theme, comes from the same source or belongs to the same genre.

◆ To present safety and health issues to children, developing their self-esteem and encouraging them to take responsibility for their own well-being.

◆ To connect with a particular time of year, or with a current event or situation.

Texts and scientific enquiry (Sc1)

As well as creating enthusiasm for science and supplying a bank of interesting and valuable information, the texts lead to opportunities for children to take part in investigative science work. They are encouraged to ask questions about living things, materials and phenomena, and to use their senses to explore and observe. Examples and ideas in the texts emphasize the importance of collecting appropriate evidence to answer a question. Children are encouraged to think about what might happen in an investigation, to recognize when a test or comparison is 'unfair', to make a simple record of what they have done, and to communicate their findings to others.

Responding to the texts

A suggested strategy for approaching a text with the children is as follows:

1. Read the piece to the children and encourage them to form their own ideas, impressions, mental pictures and emotional responses. Where it is necessary to provide some prior information, this is mentioned in the teachers' notes.

2. Ask the children for their first thoughts. Encourage them to give their opinions freely, respecting each other's ideas. Accept all suggestions and comments, showing that you value everyone's contribution.

3. Read the text again – if possible from an enlarged copy, so that the children can see the layout and follow the text. Cover up illustrations or parts of the text as appropriate.

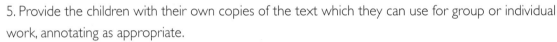

4. Ask more specific questions, relate the text to the author, discuss the purpose of the text, and identify unfamiliar words and phrases.

5. Provide the children with their own copies of the text which they can use for group or individual work, annotating as appropriate.

6. Some texts have been chosen for their performance possibilities; others are ideally suitable for children to join in and share the reading. Encourage all children to participate wherever possible.

As the text is revisited, the children's thoughts and ideas will change: images will become clearer, words and phrases will slot into place. It is not essential that every word or sentence is understood, but the breadth of the children's experience should be extended and their enjoyment increased.

Teaching with texts and the National Literacy Strategy

The texts in this book provide wide-ranging opportunities to deliver the requirements of the National Literacy Strategy at Key Stage 1:

◆ Children are presented with different genres of writing, including poetry, narrative, information, instruction, personal writing and letters. These can be used as models for their own writing.

◆ Some of the texts are extracts from a story which may be new to the children, encouraging them to read or listen to the whole of the book.

◆ Unfamiliar vocabulary in the texts leads to discussion, dictionary work and a range of activities involving words.

◆ Texts can be used as models for work on sentences, including style, punctuation and word order.

◆ All the texts encourage discussion, enabling children to develop their speaking and listening skills.

◆ Many of the texts are ideally suitable for children to enjoy as a performance.

Teaching with texts and ICT

Teachers will recognize opportunities for children to use computers with various software programs in relation to their work with texts, to support both science and literacy: writing stories, reports, instructions and labels; drawing diagrams and graphs; and finding information.

EXTRACT	GENRE	SCIENCE LEARNING OBJECTIVES	LITERACY LEARNING OBJECTIVES	PAGE
Dandelion	Poem	Sc1 1; Sc2 1c, 3a–c	◆ To compare rhyme and style with other poems. ◆ To discuss words and phrases that create effects in a poem. ◆ To use ideas for composing their own lines.	80
How to grow a giant pumpkin	Instructions	Sc1 1, 2a–j; Sc2 3a–c	◆ To recognize the importance of a sequence of instructions. ◆ To use text as a model for writing instructions.	83
Caring for your pumpkin plant	Instructions	Sc1 2f; Sc2 1c, 2b, 3a, b, 5a	◆ To identify the command words in instructions. ◆ To write a set of instructions.	86
Riddles: Plants	Riddles	Sc2 1c, 3a–c, 4b, 5a, b Breadth of study 2a	◆ To read clues to find answers. ◆ To use riddles as models for their own writing.	89

Materials

EXTRACT	GENRE	SCIENCE LEARNING OBJECTIVES	LITERACY LEARNING OBJECTIVES	PAGE
Stones	Poem with rhyme and rhythm	Sc2 1a, 5b; Sc3 1a–d	◆ To recognize the rhyme and rhythm of a poem. ◆ To write imaginatively.	94
Sorting my toys	Story	Sc3 1a–d; Sc4 2b, 3c	◆ To identify and discuss reasons for events in a story. ◆ To recognize the need for speech marks, exclamation and question marks. ◆ To recognize the importance of writing labels.	97
Introducing Flat Stanley	Introduction/ blurb and story	Sc3 1a–d, 2a	◆ To discuss shared experiences and emotions. ◆ To use an author's ideas and extend them. ◆ To write a sustained story.	100
The Snowman	Poem	Sc3 2b; Sc1 2a–j Breadth of study 2b	◆ To recognize contrasting moods created in a poem. ◆ To introduce new words and phrases. ◆ To compare with other poems on similar themes.	104
Winter Morning	Non-rhyming poem	Sc2 1b, 2b; Sc3 1d, 2b Breadth of study 2b	◆ To identify a poem which does not rhyme. ◆ To focus on words and phrases used to describe winter and ducks. ◆ To use a non-rhyming poem as a model for writing.	107
Recipes	Instructions	Sc2 2c; Sc3 1d, 2b Breadth of study 1a, 2b	◆ To recognize the usefulness of a set of instructions. ◆ To identify the command words in instructions. ◆ To compile a dictionary of related words.	110
Riddles: Materials	Riddles	Sc3 1a–d, 2b Breadth of study 2a	◆ To read clues to find answers. ◆ To use riddles as models for their own writing.	114

Physical processes

EXTRACT	GENRE	SCIENCE LEARNING OBJECTIVES	LITERACY LEARNING OBJECTIVES	PAGE
Something we cannot do without	Information	Sc4 1a, b Breadth of study 1a, b, 2b	◆ To discuss the usefulness and presentation of informative text. ◆ To create posters and labels to communicate information.	119
Christmas lights	Story	Sc4 1a–c	◆ To discuss the story theme and relate to their own experiences. ◆ To identify words relating to a theme. ◆ To write labels and instructions.	122
The Windmill	Shape poem	Sc4 2a–c	◆ To recognize structure, rhyme and presentation in a poem ◆ To identify key words and images. ◆ To use a poem as a model for their own writing.	125
Flat Stanley flies	Story	Sc3 1d; Sc4 2a–c	◆ To discuss a story theme and link it to their own experiences and emotions. ◆ To write descriptively. ◆ To use the author's ideas and continue the story.	128
The Owl Who Was Afraid of the Dark	Contents and story	Sc2 2g, 5a; Sc4 3a, b	◆ To use a contents page. ◆ To discuss and compare characters. ◆ To write a sustained story.	131
Noisy (and Quiet) Places	Nonsense poem	Sc2 2g; Sc4 3c, d	◆ To discuss how words have been selected to make a poem. ◆ To use poet's ideas to create their own writing.	135
Surrounded by Noise!	Poem with sound effects	Sc2 2g; Sc4 3c, d Breadth of study 2b	◆ To identify features of a poem. ◆ To create a performance. ◆ To use a poem as a model for their own writing.	138
Riddles: Physical processes	Riddles	Sc4 1a, 2a, 3a, b Breadth of study 2a	◆ To read clues to find answers. ◆ To use riddles as models for their own writing.	141

Humans and other animals

The texts in this chapter encourage children to ask questions about animals, including humans, and help them to begin to understand the life processes common to all living things. There are opportunities to talk about the differences between living and non-living things, and how animals' senses are important in helping them to deal with the world around them.

Animals featured in the texts range from the familiar (slugs and spiders) to the exotic (pandas and whales). Children can go on to find out about these animals' needs, the habitats they prefer and how they are suited to their environment.

Caring for babies is a focus of some of the texts. Children can consider their own infancy and that of a child in a different time and culture, as well as the early lives of other animals.

Through these texts, children are encouraged to begin to take responsibility for their own health and safety through awareness of the dangers to themselves of drugs, medicines and animals. They are also encouraged to develop a positive attitude towards all animals, and towards the environment.

Opportunities arise from the texts for children to gain first-hand experience of animals, to observe and care for them, and to group them according to their characteristics. They can investigate animal behaviour, predicting what might happen during a test, making comparisons and attempting explanations.

Brendan the traveller

Genre
story

This story about Brendan is a strange tale. Brendan was an Irish monk. He liked to travel and wanted to find out what lay beyond the sea. Brendan made many journeys over the sea in his little boat, looking for new lands.

On one of his voyages, the weary monk and his friends pulled their boat onto a small island. Using some dry wood they had brought with them, they made a fire to cook their supper.

Suddenly, Brendan and his companions were thrown into the sea. They had awoken a huge creature on whose back they had made their camp. Brendan and his friends were lucky to escape from drowning.

Some people say this story cannot be true.

Brendan the traveller

Collect pictures and a video of whales, but do not show these to the children before the first reading of the story. Allow the children to imagine the scene for themselves and talk about their ideas before you explain that the creature is supposed to have been a whale.

This story encourages children to ask questions about the world, and to consider the differences between living things and non-living things.

Science learning objectives

◆ To ask questions and decide how to find answers (Sc1 2a).
◆ To know the differences between living things and things that have never been alive (Sc2 1a).
◆ To know the senses that enable humans and other animals to be aware of the world around them (Sc2 2g).
◆ To group living things according to observable similarities and differences (Sc2 4b).

Discussing the text

◆ Give the children the opportunity to talk about what they think the huge creature might be. They might suggest a whale, a large fish or a sea monster. Eventually explain that in some versions of the story, the creature is said to be a whale.

◆ Discuss whether they think the story is true or not. Would Brendan and his friends really mistake a whale for an island? Perhaps they were tired, it was getting dark and they were just glad to get out of the boat. What clues would the children have noticed if they had been there? What would the ground have felt like beneath their feet? (Firm but springy.) Would they have mistaken it for rock? What would they have noticed was missing on the island – soil, trees, grass, animals?

◆ Why did the whale not throw them off as soon as they landed? Could it have mistaken their feet for something else – perhaps seagulls perching or waves lapping? Why would it have been woken up by the fire?

◆ Talk about the sailors' escape. How might they have saved themselves? Could the whale have eaten them?

Vocabulary

Living, alive, non-living, not alive, move, feed, grow, senses, animal, human.

Science activities

◆ Make two simple similar drawings: one of a rock in the sea (to represent an island) and one to show the back of a whale protruding from the sea. Encourage the children to tell you the differences between the two; write these as captions on the drawings. They should suggest that: the whale will move, the rock will remain still; the whale will need to feed but not the rock; the whale will grow, the rock remains the same size; the whale uses its senses to discover what is close by, the rock is unaware of anything that happens around it; the whale can reproduce but not the rock.

◆ Give groups of children a pebble and access to a small animal such as a stick insect, hamster, caterpillar or goldfish (or a bird visiting the feeding station). Ask the children to draw these two things on different pieces of paper and to show, using words, arrows and drawings, how they know that the creature is living and the pebble is not.

What senses did they use to help them? (Sight and possibly sound and smell – do not encourage them to touch the animal.)

◆ Use a video and pictures of whales to show the children where these animals live, their method of movement, their feeding habits and their family life.

◆ Ask the children to consider how a whale is similar to a human: they both move, feed, breathe, grow, reproduce and look after their young. (Explain that whales need to come to the surface to breathe.)

Further literacy ideas

◆ Look carefully at unfamiliar words in the text. Discuss their meanings and add them to the class dictionary if appropriate – for example: Irish, monk, weary, voyage, island.

◆ Identify words with similar meanings: 'small' and 'little'; 'friends' and 'companions'; 'journey' and 'voyage'. Can the children suggest another word for 'creature'?

◆ Ask the children to illustrate the stages of the story in a series of pictures: the little boat on the sea, landing, making the fire, being thrown into the sea, the escape.

◆ What happened next? The children could write Brendan's version of the escape, which he would relate when he reached home.

◆ Ask the children to enact the story, with a narrator telling the tale.

◆ Link the whale story to 'Dear Greenpeace' (page 19) and 'Jolly Blue Giant' (page 23). It could also be linked to the Biblical story of Jonah, or to the story of Pinocchio.

Pocket mouse

Colin kept a mouse in his pocket. He gave it cake crumbs and bits of cheese whenever he could. But since the mouse was simply a stuffed one that he had had since he was very small, it could not eat the food he gave it. So his pockets grew crumbier and messier as the days went by.

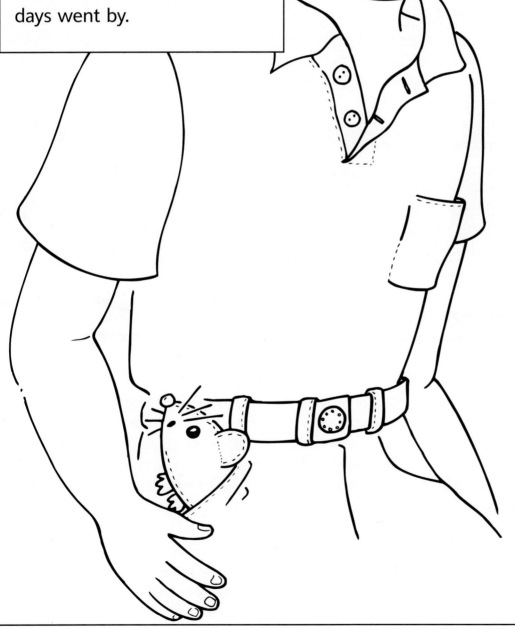

Pocket mouse

Display some pictures of mice and, if possible, a collection of toy mice.

Science learning objectives

◆ To know the differences between things that are living and things that have never been alive (Sc2 1a).

◆ To know that animals, including humans, move, feed, grow, use their senses and reproduce (Sc2 1b).

◆ To know that humans and other animals need food and water to stay alive (Sc2 2b).

◆ To know how to treat animals with care and sensitivity (Sc2 2e).

◆ To use their senses to explore and recognize the similarities and differences between materials (Sc3 1a).

Discussing the text

◆ Ask the children whether any of them have a toy – such as a teddy or doll – that they talk to and like to pretend is alive. Encourage them to relate this to Colin and his mouse. To avoid any confusion, explain that this is a stuffed toy mouse, not a stuffed real mouse such as you might see in a museum.

◆ Colin has had this mouse since he was very small. Ask the children to think which of their toys they have had the longest – perhaps something they were given as a baby. Is the toy showing signs of wear? Is it their favourite toy? How would they feel if they lost it? How would the toy feel?

◆ Talk about how Colin would know that the mouse was in his pocket without looking. He would recognize its shape and the feel of the material when he put his hand in his pocket.

Vocabulary

Living, alive, not living, healthy, food, water, grow, live, senses, materials, wood, plastic, fabric, paper.

Science activities

◆ Ask the children to suggest some advantages of having a toy mouse rather than a real mouse as a pet. (The toy will not run away, it is not messy, you can keep it for a long time, it's not harmed if you forget to look after it.)

◆ Talk about the need for a real mouse to have food and water so that it will grow and stay healthy. Point out that a mouse and a human are similar: they both need food and water to stay alive. Ask what else they both need to survive. (Air.)

◆ Make a list of foods that the children like. Then put the foods into groups such as bread, meat, fish, fruit, vegetables, cereals, cheese, sweets, drinks, biscuits and processed snack foods. Talk about the importance of eating lots of different foods to keep the body healthy and (in the case of children) to grow up strong. Point out that it is important to eat some fruit and vegetables every day, rather than eating crisps, sweets and biscuits.

◆ Collect or make toy mice of different materials such as fabric, plastic, wood, plasticine, dough and paper. Invent a game where the children take turns to feel a toy (blindfolded, or using a feely box) and identify the material. Encourage them to give reasons: 'I know this mouse is made of plastic because...'

Further literacy ideas

◆ Encourage the children to listen carefully to the sounds made by some of the words in the text, such as *mouse, pocket, cake* and *day*. Collect and link other words with the same sounds and display them prominently, perhaps with drawings: *A mouse in the house, A locket in my pocket, A cake to bake, A day to play* and so on.

◆ The children can draw and describe their own favourite toy, perhaps telling a story about its adventures.

◆ Organize a guest afternoon when each child's favourite toy is displayed and introduced to the class. The children should write a label saying who their toy is – for example, 'Hello. My name is Teddy and I have my own house.'

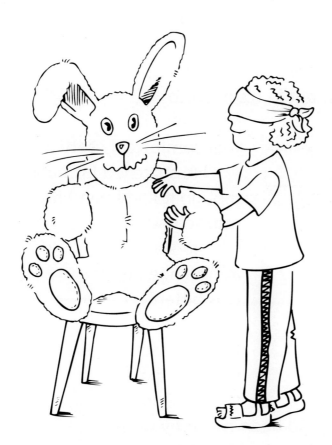

Pocket mouse 2

Genre
story

In the big field there was a great clatter as the huge red harvester was driven round and round. Nearly all the barley was cut by now. Soon Colin found himself dashing about with the farmer's son, then wrestling and rolling in the hard stubble. He got so hot that he dragged off his anorak and flung it down by the hedge. He would have left it lying there when it was time to go home, only his grandfather sent him back for it.

He fished in the pocket of his jeans for the mouse. He dropped it carefully into the pocket of his anorak, then put in his hand to make sure it was comfortably settled.

He snatched his hand out again as though it had been bitten – as though the mouse had bitten it.

He stared at his finger. It *was* bitten! There were teeth-marks so small that they looked as though they had been made by pins.

Whatever Colin had told his grandfather about the mouse not being a real one, in his pocket at this moment there was something warm and alive and furry.

Pocket mouse 2

This text emphasizes the needs of animals and how they use their senses to be aware of the world around them.

Remind the children that Colin has a toy mouse that goes everywhere with him and 'lives' in his pocket.

Science learning objectives
◆ To know the differences between things that are living and things that have never been alive (Sc2 1a).
◆ To know about the senses that enable animals to be aware of the world around them (Sc2 2g).
◆ To know how to treat animals with care and sensitivity (Sc2 2e).
◆ To recognize that there are hazards in living things (Breadth of study 2b).

Discussing the text
◆ Talk about why Colin took off his anorak, and the children's own experiences of getting hot while playing.
◆ Ask the children how they think the real mouse got into Colin's anorak pocket. Where did it come from? Perhaps it was looking for a safe, quiet, dark place because of all the noise and activity in the field. Explain that the home of the mouse was disturbed because the barley crop was being harvested.
◆ Ask the children why they think the mouse bit Colin. Point out that it was frightened and trying to protect itself. Talk about the shock to Colin when something so unexpected happened. How would he feel? Have unexpected things ever happened to any of the children? Perhaps they can recall an incident which affected the whole class.
◆ Ask the children how they would feel if they found a live mouse in their pocket.

Vocabulary
Living, not living, senses, touch, see, hear, movement.

Science activities
◆ Talk about how the mouse would use its senses. It would hear the unexpected noise, see movement and become frightened; it would find its way into a narrow space using its sense of touch (the whiskers). Compare the live mouse with the toy mouse in the pocket of Colin's jeans. The toy mouse would be unaware of the activity and noise. It would not get hot or frightened while Colin was racing around.
◆ Remind the children that it is important to respect the needs of animals. Pets must be treated kindly and provided with food, water and a suitable home. Wild animals can be observed carefully but need to be left alone: they should never be disturbed, hurt or removed from their homes. Discuss appropriate examples – perhaps animals the children might find, such as frogs and their spawn, fish in streams and birds on their nests. Explain that wild animals do not benefit from captivity: it is better to leave them alone to live their lives in their natural surroundings where they have the best chance of survival. Mention the need to conserve the habitats of wild animals.

◆ The children can draw a real mouse and a toy mouse and record the differences between them on a chart (see illustration below).

◆ Point out that Colin and the mouse would be using the same senses in the cornfield to see the movements and hear the sounds of people and machinery and to feel and smell the straw, the ground and other animals. However, they will not sense things in quite the same way – for example, the mouse has a better sense of smell and its whiskers are more sensitive to touch than Colin's hands; but Colin probably has better eyesight.

Further literacy ideas

◆ Underline and list words in the text that indicate quick movements: *dashing, wrestling, rolling, dragged off, flung, snatched.* Ask the children to extend this list with words of their own. Add these to the class dictionary if appropriate.

◆ What happened next? The children can write their own version of the next part of the story. Ask them to think about what they would do if they found a live mouse in their pocket.

◆ Focus on opposites and the contrasting situations in the story: bright – dark or shady; movement – stillness; hot – cool.

real mouse

- needs food and water
- can run about
- needs air to breathe
- can hear noises
- uses whiskers to feel its way around

pocket mouse

- does not need food or water
- cannot run about
- does not need air, does not breathe
- cannot hear any noises

Dear Greenpeace

Dear Greenpeace,

    I love whales very much and I think I saw one in my pond to-day. Please send me some information on whales, as I think he might be hurt.

        love

          Emily

Whale

Dear Emily,

    Here are some details about whales. I don't think you'll find it was a whale you saw, because whales don't live in ponds, but in salt water.

    Yours sincerely,

    Greenpeace

Dear Greenpeace,

Tonight I am very happy because I saw my whale jump up and spurt lots of water. He looked blue.

Does this mean he might be a blue whale?

love Emily

P.S. What can I feed him with?

Dear Emily,

Blue whales are blue and they eat tiny shrimp-like creatures that live in the sea. However I must tell you that a blue whale is much too big to live in your pond.

Yours sincerely,

Greenpeace

P.S. Perhaps it is a blue goldfish?

Dear Greenpeace

Collect photographs and books showing pond and sea creatures. Explain that Greenpeace is a group of people that tries to take care of the Earth and all the plants and animals that live on it.

These letters encourage the children to think and ask questions about the world around them.

Science learning objectives

◆ To be aware that it is important to collect evidence... when trying to answer a question (Sc1 1).

◆ To relate life processes to animals and plants found in the local environment (Sc2 1c).

◆ To know that humans and animals need food and water to stay alive (Sc2 2b).

◆ To know how to treat animals with care and sensitivity (Sc2 2e).

◆ To group living things according to observable similarities and differences (Sc2 4b).

◆ To use a range of environmental contexts that are familiar and interesting (Breadth of study 1a).

Discussing the text

◆ Establish who is writing each letter and who is receiving it. Ask what sort of person the children think Emily is. What do they think of the replies from Greenpeace?

◆ Discuss whether Emily really did see a whale. Allow individuals their own opinions at this stage.

◆ Why is the Greenpeace writer sure that there cannot be a whale in the pond? Can the children think of any other reasons? (Whales live in salt water; a whale is too big to live in a pond; a whale could not have found its way to the pond; there would not be the right food in the pond.)

◆ Is there such a thing as a blue goldfish? Has anyone seen one? Perhaps the Greenpeace writer is joking. Create an air of mystery surrounding the idea of a blue goldfish.

◆ Ask the children to tell you all they know about whales, including what they have discovered from the letters. Write down this information on a poster for display.

Vocabulary

Live, grow, animal, creature, whale, goldfish, swim, human, habitat, size, large, small, protect, similar, different.

Science activities

◆ Establish the type of habitat a whale requires and discuss how this differs from the habitat provided by a pond in terms of size, type of water and food available. Talk about the need for whales to meet other whales and the amount of water required for diving and travelling. The children can record the contrasting needs of a goldfish and of a blue whale, using drawings and sentences.

◆ Ask the children to say what kind of animals might be found in a pond and which is likely to be the biggest of these. If appropriate, organize a pond-dipping session to show the children the range and quantity of small creatures living in the water. You will need transparent containers for collecting samples of water, tanks or shallow trays for observing and hand lenses or other magnifiers. Working in groups, the children can record the creatures found in samples of water taken from different parts of the pond (such as the sunny side, the shady side, the surface water, the deeper water). Make a simple column graph to represent the creatures seen in each sample of water. It is not necessary to identify every specimen accurately, and making up appropriate names for unknown creatures is acceptable.

◆ Remind the children that a whale and a human are both animals and discuss ways in which they are similar: both need to feed, grow, move about and reproduce.

◆ Compare a whale with another animal that spends all its life in water, such as a goldfish: both swim well with the help of their tails, have no legs, and would die if removed from water.

◆ Talk about the need for animals to live in the most suitable habitat, where they can find shelter and food, meet other animals of the same kind and reproduce. Take this opportunity to tell the children that creatures of any kind should not be removed from their natural habitat without very good reason, and animals collected for observation should be treated properly and returned to where they were found as soon as possible. Discuss which animals can be kept as pets ('domesticated' animals that have been specifically bred for this purpose) and which are best left to live in the wild (all wild animals).

◆ The children can each draw a creature on a card and draw its habitat on another card, then use the set of cards for a matching game.

Further literacy ideas

◆ Ask half the class to represent Emily and read out her letters, with the other children reading the replies.

◆ Discuss what is missing from these letters that you would normally expect to see: date, address. What conventions of letter-writing do these letters show?

◆ Encourage the children to continue the exchange of letters, perhaps composing a class or group letter from Emily with an adult or another group of children replying on behalf of Greenpeace. The problem of feeding or removing the 'whale' might be suggested. Will the ending be happy or sad? Provide envelopes for the children to address and post (using a class post-box). Display the letters in sequence, so that the children can enjoy rereading them.

◆ The children can find out about people who work to protect whales, or look at brochures that advertise whale-watching holidays.

◆ Ask the children to choose an animal they would like to help and protect. They can record their ideas and feelings for others to read, or give a presentation during an assembly.

Genre
humorous
poem

Jolly Blue Giant

The Blue's the biggest kind of Whale
At thirty metres, top to tail.
The largest creature on the earth
(It's seven metres long at birth!)
And as for weight, it's twenty-five
Times any elephant alive.
If you should meet one face to face,
You need not swim away apace
In fear, or even show alarm,
The Blue won't do you any harm.
It isn't that Blue Whales are wimps.
It's just that all they eat is shrimps.

Dick King-Smith

Jolly Blue Giant

This poem interests children in the wider world by describing a spectacular animal.

Collect books, pictures and videos showing different types of whale.

Science learning objectives

◆ To know that animals, including humans, move, feed, grow, use their senses and reproduce (Sc2 1b).

◆ To group living things according to observable similarities and differences (Sc2 4b).

◆ To use a range of environmental contexts that are familiar and interesting (Breadth of study 1a).

Discussing the text

◆ Encourage the children to enjoy the rhyme and rhythm of the poem. Read out the lines several times while talking about the content.

◆ Help the children to appreciate the dimensions of the blue whale by comparing its length with that of the room. Explain that there has never been an animal on Earth bigger than this type of whale, not even in the days of the dinosaurs.

◆ Perhaps the children associate size with fierceness. According to the poem, why is there no need to be afraid of the blue whale?

◆ In the title, Dick King-Smith describes the whale as 'jolly'. Ask the children what this word means. Would they think of describing a creature like a whale as jolly? Perhaps the poet wants us to think of the whale as a friendly and happy creature that would not hurt us. Do the children believe him?

◆ Discuss the likelihood of coming face to face with a blue whale. What creatures would the children definitely not want to come face to face with?

Vocabulary

Alive, live, home, habitat, animal, human, whale, shrimp, feed, move, have young, big, bigger, biggest, long, longer, longest.

Science activities

◆ Find out whether all types of whales eat the same kind of food. Why do some whales have teeth? Discuss the amount of food that such huge creatures need to stay alive and grow.

◆ With the children's help, measure out thirty metres and seven metres on the playground to show the lengths of an adult and a baby blue whale respectively. If all the children hold hands and stretch out, can they reach from the head to the tail?

◆ Show a video of a whale and ask the children to describe its movement. Which parts of a whale's body are involved with movement? Is the whale's movement anything like a human's?

◆ Discuss which senses might be most useful to whales. Tell the children that scientists are still trying to explain how whales find their way around the world's oceans.

◆ Show pictures and a video of a whale and its young. Discuss how the way that a mother whale looks after its baby is similar and different to the way humans look after their young. Note that both human and whale mothers keep close to their babies, keep them out of danger and show them around.

◆ Provide pictures of other animals that live in the sea (such as the dolphin, octopus, crab and various types of fish and shellfish), and ask the children to group them according to observable features. For example, they could sort the animals into those with legs and those with none; or those with a soft body and those with a hard covering.

◆ The children can create an information sheet or booklet on the features and activities of whales. Then, as whale experts, they can share their knowledge with another class.

Further literacy ideas

◆ Cover the last word of each line and ask the children to join in with the right word as you read out the poem again.

◆ The children can copy out the rhyming words onto small cards, mix these up and then challenge each other to match them again.

◆ After several readings, some children will remember a line and be confident enough to repeat it for the class. Organize a line of six or twelve children to perform the poem.

◆ Talk about the words *big, bigger, biggest* and encourage the children to use these to compare different animals: *A dog is big. An elephant is bigger. A whale is the biggest.* Ask the children to make sentences using the words *long, longer, longest* in relation to a stick insect, a grass snake and a whale.

Favourite foods

Genre
spoken words

Moving around

Genre
spoken words

I can run quite fast when I need to get somewhere.

I move around in the tunnels I have dug under the ground.

I scamper up and down tree trunks and jump from branch to branch.

I fly at night, fluttering between the treetops.

I hop about in the fields, but I can run fast when I need to.

I walk slowly about the fields and woods at night.

I am a very fast runner but I can also creep about very quietly.

I climb up the stems of plants, and can squeeze through very small gaps.

Homes for babies

Genre
spoken words

I choose a safe place under a shed or in a pile of warm leaves.

My babies are safe in my cosy tunnels.

My babies hold onto to me as I hang upside-down under a roof or inside a hollow tree.

I dig burrows in banks so that my babies can be safe underground.

I make a nest out of twigs for my babies, high in a tree.

I always dig a large hole among the roots of a tree, where my babies will be safe.

I find a hole in a bank and make it bigger for my babies.

I use leaves and stems to weave a nest for my babies.

Favourite foods/Moving around/Homes for babies

These spoken words remind children of the feeding, movement and homes of a number of similar animals that share an environment.

Display further pictures of the animals shown on the photocopiable pages.

Science learning objectives

◆ To know that animals, including humans, move, feed, grow, use their senses and reproduce (Sc2 1b).

◆ To know that humans and other animals need food and water to stay alive (Sc2 2b).

◆ To know that humans and other animals can produce offspring and that these offspring grow into adults (Sc2 2f).

◆ To group living things according to observable similarities and differences (Sc2 4b).

◆ To use a range of environmental contexts that are familiar and interesting (Breadth of study 1a).

Discussing the text

Focus on one set of spoken words at a time.

◆ Find out whether the children can recognize each of these animals from pictures. Ask them whether these animals have anything in common; they may notice that the animals all have a furry covering (though most of the hedgehog's covering is spines), have four legs and live in the wild.

◆ For 'Favourite foods', highlight the key words that tell us what each animal likes to eat – slugs, earthworms, insects, nuts, grass, earthworms and bulbs, berries and acorns, rabbits and leftovers.

◆ For 'Moving around', ask questions to help the children become familiar with the animals' movements, such as: *Which are the fast runners? Which are the good climbers? Which of these animals can fly?*

◆ For 'Homes for babies', ask questions about the animals' young: *Which babies spend their early life underground? Which babies live in a high place?*

Vocabulary

Similar, different, food, feeding, move, moving, movement, baby, babies, young, homes.

Science activities

◆ Can the children describe a habitat where all these creatures might be found, such as a countryside area with woodland and fields? Which of the animals are the children most likely to see in the wild? Is it possible that some of them visit the school grounds when everyone has gone home? Children in an urban environment can consider whether any of these animals can be found in a town (perhaps the fox and squirrel). Give each child an outline of a countryside scene, onto which drawings of the animals and labels can be added.

◆ Can the children link the movement of each animal to the food it eats? The squirrel is a good climber, so it can reach nuts on a tree. The fox runs fast, so it can catch a rabbit. The bat can fly, so it can catch flying insects.

◆ Point out that all of these animals look after their babies. Make a list of other animals, including humans, that care for their young; talk about animals that do not, such as the frog and the butterfly.

◆ Choose other animals from a quite different environment and encourage the children to write down words they might use to describe these animals' activities – for example, a snake, a fish and a bird in the riverside environment.

Further literacy ideas

◆ Write the names of the animals on cards for the children to match with their pictures.

◆ Provide pictures of the animals for the children to match with words describing their food and movement.

◆ Discuss the convention of speech bubbles. How else can speech be represented? (Picture captions, speech marks.)

◆ The children can choose one animal and cut its picture and speech bubble from each page to make a simple information card. Display these, and encourage the children to read them to each other. Other information about the animals can be added to the cards if appropriate. The children can write a description of the appearance of the creature they have chosen – for example, 'I am black and white with a stripy head' for the badger.

◆ Collect words describing movement, such as *creep, scamper* and *fly*, and create a class dictionary or word book about ways of moving around.

Did you really?

Genre
rhymed poem

I saw a ball roll down a grassy slope,
I saw a ladybird crawl along a rope.

I saw a drop of water trickle down the window-pane,
I saw a fieldmouse run along a country lane.

I saw a candle flame flickering by the door,
I saw a spider creep across the floor.

I saw a cloud drift across the sky,
I saw a baby robin learning how to fly.

I saw the moon wink its eye at me,
And I saw a golden eagle eat my brother's tea.

Did you really?

This poem encourages children to record their observations of the movements of living things and non-living things.

Display pictures to stimulate the children's awareness of the activity of animals and the movement of non-living things (such as rivers and smoke).

Science learning objectives

◆ To explore, using the senses of sight and hearing, and make and record observations (Sc1 2f).

◆ To know the differences between things that are living and things that have never been alive (Sc2 1a).

◆ To know about the senses that enable humans and other animals to be aware of the world around them (Sc2 2g).

◆ To find out about, and describe, the movement of familiar things (Sc4 2a).

Discussing the text

◆ Ask the children how they know that this is a poem. They may suggest: because it rhymes, because it has repetition, because each sentence is on a new line, or because there are spaces between some of the lines.

◆ Underline the rhyming words. Ask one group of children to repeat the first word of each pair, with another group following on with the rhyme.

◆ Read only the second line of each couplet. Ask the children to say what the things described there have in common (they are alive), and how they are different from the things described in the first lines (which are not alive).

◆ What do the children think about the last two lines of the poem? Are they just as likely to see the things described here as those in the rest of the poem?

Vocabulary

Living, not living, senses, see, saw, hear, heard, movements.

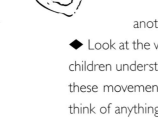

Science activities

◆ Ask the children to list and draw the things in the poem that are living, then those that are not living.

◆ Consider the movements of the living creatures: crawl, run, creep, fly, eat. Ask the children to describe other movements that animals make. Invent a simple oral game in which one child names (or reads the name of) an animal and another replies with the appropriate movement.

◆ Look at the words that describe the movements of things that are not alive. Find out whether the children understand the meaning of each word. Can they think of other non-living things that display these movements? The children can make lists of things that roll, trickle, flicker and drift. Can they think of anything non-living that really does wink? They may suggest a warning light.

◆ Take the children outside. Ask them to keep quiet and to look around carefully for a few minutes. Tell them that you want them to spot something which others might not have seen, and yet which could be quite ordinary. Afterwards, ask the children to tell each other what they saw. Explain how useful it is to be able to notice details that help us to learn things about our surroundings.

◆ On another occasion, ask the children to listen very carefully and record the things that they have heard; then ask them to group the sounds into those made by living things and those made by non-living things.

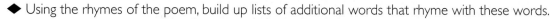

Further literacy ideas

◆ Encourage the children to use the poem as a model and create some lines of their own that begin: 'I saw...'. Create a class poem, using a line from each child. Consider any rhymes a bonus.

◆ On a visit to a different environment (such as a wood, a seashore or a town), encourage the children to close their eyes and listen for any unusual sounds. Talk about what they have heard, and help them to create some lines that begin: 'I heard...'.

◆ Using the rhymes of the poem, build up lists of additional words that rhyme with these words.

◆ Focus on the words *drop, slope, spider* and *fly* – what do they have in common? Encourage the children to find other words that begin in the same way.

Feeting the birds

Genre
diary

Saturday: We put some seed on the bird table and hung up a bag of nuts. Skipper, our cat, wondered what we were doing.

Sunday: Skipper and I watched all day from my window but no birds came to our feeding station.

Monday: Today, while Skipper was asleep, a blue tit pecked the nuts and a robin ate some of the seed.

Tuesday: Every time Skipper and I looked out of the window, a blue tit was clinging to the nuts.

Wednesday: Lots of starlings flew down to eat the seed today. They frightened all the little birds away. When Skipper walked down the garden, the starlings flew away.

Thursday: A robin has been trying to eat the nuts but it cannot cling onto the bag like the blue tits can. Sometimes the robin waits on the ground and pecks up any pieces of nut the blue tits drop.

Friday: It was raining. Skipper stayed inside all day. Two doves visited our bird table, as well as the robin and some blue tits.

Saturday: A black and white bird with red patches came to eat the nuts today. I am wondering what sort of a bird it is.

Sunday: All the nuts have gone. We will have to buy some more bird food, as well as cat food, when we go to the shops. Mum says the animals cost more to feed than I do.

Feeding the birds

Display pictures of some familiar birds (such as a blue tit, great tit, robin, blackbird, starling, chaffinch and sparrow) that might visit a garden bird table. Have reference books on British birds available.

The text provides a model to show how a diary of observations could be written.

Science teaching objectives

◆ To use first-hand experience and simple information sources to answer questions (Sc1 2b).

◆ To make and record observations (Sc1 2f).

◆ To communicate what happened in a variety of ways (Sc1 2g).

◆ To explain what happened, drawing on their knowledge and understanding (Sc1 2i).

◆ To know that humans and other animals need food and water to stay alive (Sc2 2b).

◆ To group living things according to observable similarities and differences (Sc2 4b).

◆ To find out about the different kinds of animals in the local environment (Sc2 5a).

Discussing the text

◆ Ask the children what kind of text this is. Do they recognize it as a diary? Ask what clues indicate this. Establish that a record has been made every day for nine days.

◆ Can the children suggest why the birds did not visit the bird table during the first two days? Perhaps they had not noticed the food by then. Perhaps they saw the observer and the cat, and were afraid. Talk about the idea of 'getting used' to things.

◆ Ask the children to name the different birds mentioned, and to underline each bird's name in a different colour on the sheet.

◆ Talk about who frightens whom. The starlings frighten the smaller birds; the cat frightens all the birds, including the starlings.

◆ Do the children have any idea what the unknown bird described in the text might be? Accept all suggestions but do not confirm any of them. Ask the children how they could find out the answer later.

Vocabulary

Food, feeding, see, watch, observe, bird, feathers, wing, fly.

Science activities

◆ Display pictures of the birds mentioned in the diary. Ask the children how they recognize each of them: the robin has a red breast, the blue tit is small with a blue head and tail, and so on. What other birds would the children expect to see feeding in a local garden? They might suggest blackbird, sparrow, great tit. Provide a selection of pictures and books about common birds so that the children can discover that the mystery bird in the diary is probably a great spotted woodpecker.

◆ Encourage the children to write their own diary of observations. If appropriate, set up a feeding station that can be seen from a classroom window. If the children's movements scare away the birds,

cover the window with paper in which spy holes have been cut. Alternatively, the children can make regular observations of the movements and feeding habits of a mouse, hamster or gerbil.

◆ Ask the children to explain any points of interest in their diary entries. They can make a chart or a graph to show the birds seen each day.

◆ Discuss how all birds are similar: they have feathers, wings and beaks, they lay eggs, most of them can fly.

Further literacy ideas

◆ Find the words in the text that describe the activities of the birds: pecked, ate, clinging, flew. Collect other words appropriate to birds.

◆ Encourage the children to make a picture dictionary of birds.

◆ Allow time towards the end of each day (or each week) for the children to add an entry to a class or individual diary.

Silverfish, Spiders and Flies

Genre
rhymed poem

Small creatures see
That none of the space
In our classroom
Goes to waste.

Silverfish keep warm
In cracks too small
Even for children's fingers
In the floor and against the wall.

And knitting their webs
The spiders fit
Onto ledges too narrow
For children to sit.

Flies stand on the ceiling
Or circle through the air
And even in PE
I never climbed up there.

Creatures that look
Like pips and seeds
Sow themselves in the places
No-one else needs.

Stanley Cook

Silverfish, spiders and Flies

This poem encourages children to think about some of the small animals with which they share their immediate environment.

You might like to collect some silverfish for the children to observe. They can be kept for a few days in a transparent container with a moistened paper towel, and fed on breadcrumbs. Display magnified photographs and pictures of minibeasts; if possible, show a video to demonstrate their movements.

Science learning objectives

◆ To predict what might happen before deciding what to do (Sc1 2c).
◆ To explore, using the sense of sight... and make and record observations (Sc1 2f).
◆ To compare what happened with what was predicted, and try to explain it, drawing on knowledge and understanding (Sc1 2i).
◆ To know that animals move, feed, grow, use their senses and reproduce (Sc2 1b).
◆ To find out about the different kinds of animals in the local environment (Sc2 5a).

Discussing the text

◆ Spiders and flies should be familiar to all the children – but have any of them seen a silverfish? Explain that these creatures hide away in dark corners and move very fast, so they are rarely seen. Can the children explain why they should be called 'silverfish' when they do not live in water? (They are covered with silvery scales and are fish-shaped.)

◆ Talk about the advantages of being very small and so being able to move about in the tiny cracks and spaces of a room. Where would the children choose to explore?

◆ Encourage the children to look at the last verse and spot words that are usually used when talking about plants: *pips, seeds, sow*. Why do they think Stanley Cook uses these words? Perhaps the tiny creatures remind him of seeds when they are very still – and like seeds, they are easy to ignore until they show signs of life.

Vocabulary

Live, living, creatures, habitat, warm, cool, dark, bright.

Science activities

◆ Make sure that the children can identify each creature illustrated on the sheet and relate it to the appropriate verse of the poem.

◆ Compile an information poster or booklet for each of the three creatures. The children can provide drawings, captions and sentences, and add to the information as they find things out. Include information on how each animal moves, what it eats, what sort of place it prefers to live in, and whether it has any enemies. Explain that flies and silverfish are seen as pests because they spread germs but spiders perform a useful job in catching and eating flies.

◆ Encourage the children to predict what creatures might be sharing the classroom with them and where they might be living, then carry out a survey. (Obtain the caretaker's permission before arranging this.) They should look in cupboards, behind bookcases, in boxes and quiet corners, on plants, under carpets and up at the ceiling. Emphasize that the animal hunt must be performed quietly and carefully, so as not to frighten away or disturb the creatures. Point out the importance of careful observation when carrying out a scientific task.

Record the children's findings on a chart (see illustration below). Discuss why the places where creatures were found are good habitats: *Are they warm, cool, dark or bright? Do they provide shelter from enemies, or a good place to hunt for food?* Encourage the children to try to explain what they have found out from their survey. Woodlice and silverfish like to be where it is dark. Greenfly are only found on plants. Spiders do not mind being out in the open.

Further literacy ideas

◆ Ask the children to provide opposites for adjectives in the poem such as *small, warm* and *narrow*. Make a list of other opposites they might know.

◆ Find verbs to describe the activities of silverfish (*creep, scurry, dodge, hide*), spiders (*crawl, dangle, cling, pounce*) and flies (*circle, walk, buzz, climb*).

◆ The children can imagine the life of a small creature in the classroom, and write how that creature feels about sharing the room with people.

◆ Look at the rhymes in the poem. Ask the children to find more rhymes with the same spelling patterns: seeds, needs, feeds, weeds; small, wall, tall, hall; and so on.

minibeasts	habitats	our comments
woodlice	under plant pot under door mat	They like dark, damp places.
greenfly	pot plants on window sill	Greenfly feed on plant juices.
spiders	corner of window ceiling lights behind door on pot plant	Spiders like to be everywhere.
silverfish	store cupboard	Silverfish run away quickly when we open the door.
ladybird	potted plant	We think the ladybird has discovered the greenfly on our plants.

Genre
Humorous
information
text

Dare YOU make friends with... an ugly slug?

by Nick Arnold

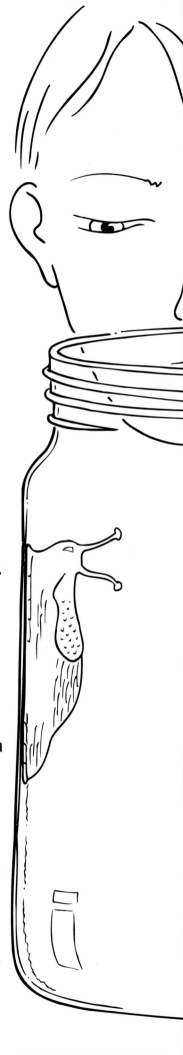

Here's how to snuggle up to a slug. Who knows, you could be in for a horribly interesting encounter!

1 First meet your slug. You can tell where there are slugs around by the horrible silvery slime trails they leave. They like to slither about in the open on warm damp summer evenings. So just follow a tempting trail until you find your slug lurking under the leaves of a small plant.

2 Enjoy that gooey, squelchy feel between your fingers as you put your slug in a glass jar.

3 Watch in amazement as your ugly slug climbs the slippery walls of the jar. It moves on a layer of slime produced by its foot. The sticky slime allows the slug to cling to the glass. Waves of movement push its foot forward. Think about it – could you climb up a glass wall on just one foot that's been dipped in something rather like raw egg?

4 Imagine you were a bird. Would you want to eat the slug? Not likely – the slime tastes disgusting! But hedgehogs think they are horribly delicious.

5 Put your new friend back where you found him/her. That way you'll stay friends.

Dare YOU make friends with... an ugly slug?

Display enlarged pictures of slugs and obtain a video to show slug movement in close-up.

Science learning objectives

◆ To collect evidence by making observations and measurements when trying to answer a question (Sc1 1).

◆ To develop investigative skills through a complete investigation (Sc1 2a–j).

◆ To know that animals move, feed, grow, use their senses and reproduce (Sc2 1b).

◆ To relate life processes to animals and plants found in the local environment (Sc2 1c).

◆ To group living things according to observable similarities and differences (Sc2 4b).

◆ To identify similarities and differences between local environments and ways in which these affect animals and plants that are found there (Sc2 5b).

Discussing the text

◆ How does Nick Arnold feel about slugs? Do the children think he likes them? He seems to know a lot about them so he must have made friends with them himself! Do the children share his feelings for slugs? Do they agree that slugs are ugly?

◆ What do the children think 'encounter' means? Have they heard this word before?

◆ Ask the children whether they personally would like to follow the instructions for making friends with a slug. Refer to the numbered points when discussing this so the children can begin to understand the usefulness of information written in this way.

◆ Focus on point **2** in the text. Consider whether Nick Arnold really expects us to touch slugs. Perhaps he is just trying to make us shiver and squirm. Talk about ways of avoiding touching slugs with bare hands, such as wearing gloves or tempting the slug onto a leaf.

◆ Talk about some of the words and phrases used to describe slugs and their activities. Ask the children to pick out some of their favourites, such as *horrible silvery slime trails* or *that gooey, squelchy feel*.

Vocabulary

Animals, feed, grow, shelter, leaves, senses, observe, observations, evidence.

Science activities

◆ Show the children how to handle slugs for observation without actually touching them with their fingers: use a paintbrush, a strong leaf or a piece of paper to transfer the slugs.

◆ Keep some slugs in a transparent container for a few days so that the children can make observations. Make sure that the slugs have some fresh leaves as food, a wet paper towel to provide damp conditions and stones for shelter. The children can each write a sentence describing what they see for a class diary. Encourage them to notice the slugs' structure, movement and feeding habits.

◆ Organize a complete investigation to find out which foods slugs prefer. Ask the children for ideas about how they could find out whether slugs have a favourite food. They will need to make the test as fair as possible so that the results will be meaningful. The children might suggest arranging leaves and pieces of vegetables of different kinds in a suitable container and allowing a hungry slug to make its choice. Talk about the value of trying several slugs, as a single slug cannot be relied upon to provide sufficient evidence. Decide what factors must remain the same for each trial (for example: the types of food, the way the slugs are introduced into the container, the type of slug, the length of time the slugs are allowed to feed). Covering the container with black paper will encourage the slugs to feed.

Insist on careful observation and recording – perhaps noting how many slugs are eating each type of food after every 10 minutes. Encourage the children to talk about their results. Make a large chart to show the slugs' preferences. Explain that as the test was carried out fairly, the results are valuable. Point out how these results might be useful to gardeners whose crops slugs like to eat, as they will know which plants to protect; if there are plants that slugs avoid, these could be planted around the slugs' favourite plants to trick the slugs into leaving the latter alone.

◆ Provide appropriate books and pictures so that the children can find out what animals are similar to slugs. They can make a series of labelled drawings to show these; they should include different kinds of land snails, sea slugs and sea snails. Encourage them to give reasons for putting these animals into one group – for example: they have soft bodies, they do not have legs, they like to live in damp places. If appropriate, introduce the term 'mollusc': an animal with a soft body (covered with slime) and a single foot.

◆ If appropriate, take the children on a slug hunt. Ask them to predict, using their knowledge of the habits of these creatures, where they will find the most slugs. Prepare a simple class chart to bring together the information collected; record the numbers and perhaps the types of slugs found (such as large black slugs and small brown slugs). Talk about why slugs are found in particular places (usually where it is dark and damp), and what animals are their enemies.

Further literacy ideas

◆ Look carefully at the words *slug*, *ugly* and *snuggle*, and collect other words with the same sound. Perhaps the children can compose a simple nonsense rhyme using words such as *snug*, *bug*, *rug* and *hug*.

◆ Make a collection of words beginning with *sl*, including those found in the text: *slug*, *slither*, *slime*.

◆ Ask the children to look at point 1 in the text and find examples of words that begin with the same sound and come together (such as *silvery slime* and *tempting trail*).

◆ Talk about the way the writer is telling us what to do, giving an instruction in each point: **1** meet (the slug), **2** enjoy (the feel); **3** watch (in amazement); **4** imagine (you are a bird); **5** put (your new friend back). Ask the children to write a simple set of instructions for others to use – for example, saying how to care for a pet or a growing plant.

◆ Ask the children to write some sentences about 'My friend the slug'.

The Giant Panda 1

Genre
Story

One bright day, the panda sniffs around a little cave she has found. It seems warm and dry. She pulls in twigs, bamboo stems and fir branches to make a bed. Then she settles down, blocking the entrance with her body to keep the cave snug and safe.

Here, the panda has her baby cub. At first he is tiny, blind and helpless. But he soon grows, nourished by his mother's rich, warm milk.

     43

The Giant Panda 2

Genre
Information
text

● Pandas **mostly have twins**, but only one cub usually lives. A panda may give birth to eight or nine cubs in her lifetime.

newborn
small and pink,
cannot see, weighs
just 100 grams

3 weeks
black-and-white
markings show

10 weeks
eyes now open,
mother may carry it
gently in her mouth

● A **baby panda's skin** is dark where the black fur will grow and pale where the white fur will grow.

3 months
starts to crawl

6 months
starts to eat bamboo

1 year
can walk quite well,
teeth have come through

● Pandas live until they are about **25 to 30 years old**.

The Giant Panda

Display pictures and books showing pandas and how they live. If possible, collect some bamboo stems or borrow a potted bamboo plant.

This extract describes the birth and care of a baby panda, both in narrative form and as information text.

Science learning objectives

◆ To know that humans and other animals can produce offspring and that these offspring grow into adults (Sc2 2f).

◆ To know about the senses that enable humans and other animals to be aware of the world around them (Sc2 2g).

Discussing the text

◆ Elicit the children's feelings about pandas. What is it about these animals that makes them so appealing? Talk about how the children feel about other animals that they do not like as much. If appropriate, compare with their reaction to slugs (see pages 40–2).

◆ Discuss what kind of home the panda in the story wanted for her baby, and how she made sure it was suitable.

◆ Help the children to identify differences between the two pieces of writing about pandas. There is a story that tells us what might have happened to one panda, and a section of information about all pandas.

◆ Explain that bamboo leaves are the main food of pandas, and that 'nourished' means 'provided with suitable healthy food'. Children are *nourished* during the day by a school dinner or a packed lunch.

◆ Give the children the opportunity to feel 100 grams, perhaps by holding a small book, so that they can appreciate the weight of a newborn panda.

Vocabulary

Baby, babies, mother, birth, senses, see, hear, taste, smell.

Science activities

◆ This activity can be carried out by groups or the whole class. Create a timeline divided into months to represent a year. Above the line, record the events in the life of a panda as stated in the text. Below the line, record the development of a human baby. (See illustration on page 46.) Children with babies in the family can provide first-hand information about how babies feed and when they crawl and walk. Other children can ask their parents about themselves as babies. Use the completed timeline to find similarities and differences between the development of a panda baby and that of a human baby.

◆ Point out that pandas and humans are both animals, and are similar in many ways: they move, feed, grow and reproduce but they live in different environments. The children can collect together all the information they have found about pandas and contribute to a class book.

◆ Remind the children that a newborn panda is 'tiny, blind and helpless'. Encourage them to think about how the animal's senses help it to learn about the world around it as it grows up. While blind, it probably uses its sense of smell to recognize its mother, and will feel the warmth of her body on its skin. As its eyes open, it will see its mother, its home and later the outside world. The baby will get to know the taste of the mother's milk and then the bamboo leaves. Some sounds will become familiar, but anything unusual will warn of danger. Refer to a human baby growing up and using the senses of sight, smell, touch, hearing and taste to learn about new things.

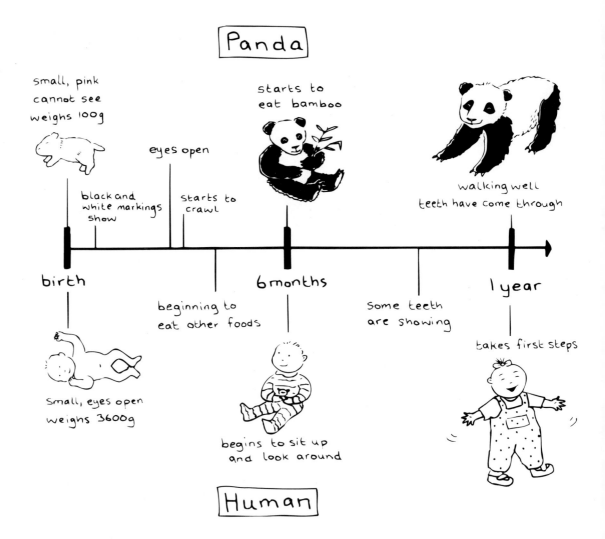

Further literacy ideas

◆ The text provides an opportunity for the children to identify and list words beginning with the letter 'b': *bright, bamboo, branches, bed, blocking, body, baby, blind, black* and *birth* – also *but* and *by*. They could list these words in alphabetical order, using the second (or even third) letter.

◆ Ask the children to write a description of a panda for someone who has never seen a picture of this animal.

◆ Make 'nourished' the word of the week, and use it frequently. Give children credit if they can bring it into other conversations.

◆ Encourage the children to continue the story of the baby panda as it grows up and finds its way around its environment. Point out that the passage of information text should be useful for this.

The Gift

The Gift from Winklesea had come into the lives of the Kane family like a shooting star, brushed their lives with magic, and vanished. He had hatched out of what they had thought was an egg-shaped stone. It was a bluish green, and mounted on a cockleshell pedestal. Dan and Mary had brought it back from a day at Winklesea as a gift for their mother.

The odd, sleek grey little creature that had hatched out of it had turned out to be a gift for the whole family. He had ended up, in fact, as one of the family.

'Don't you remember the actual night he hatched out?' said Mary. 'While we were having our fish and chips?'

'On the mantlepiece it was,' said Mrs Kane. 'Between the clock and the green glass cat.'

'And he scooted straight behind the clock,' said Dan. 'And then peered out at us.'

'Frightened to death, poor little lamb!' cried Mrs Kane.

'Ah, but we soon tamed him, mother,' Mr Kane reminded her. 'It was the chips that did it. *My* idea to give him a chip, I seem to remember.'

(from **Whatever Happened In Winklesea** by Helen Cresswell)

The Gift

This text sets the scene for a story about a strange creature that has hatched from an egg.

Collect pictures of eggs and the animals that hatch from them. Draw some different-sized eggs to scale, ranging from that of a wren to that of an ostrich. The actual dimensions are as follows: hen 6cm × 4.5cm; wren 2cm long; ostrich 20cm × 15cm; mute swan (the largest egg laid by a British nesting bird) 11.4 cm × 7.3cm; golden eagle 8cm × 5cm; chiffchaff 1.6cm long. Display a collection of pebbles and egg-like stones along with hen's eggs and eggshells.

Science learning objectives

◆ To collect evidence by making observations when trying to answer a question (Sc1 1).

◆ To know the differences between things that are living and things that have never been alive (Sc2 1a).

◆ To know that humans and other animals need food and water to stay alive (Sc2 2b).

◆ To know how to treat animals with care and sensitivity (Sc2 2e).

◆ To know that humans and other animals can produce offspring and that these offspring grow into adults (Sc2 2f).

Discussing the text

◆ Talk about bringing back souvenirs from a holiday or day out to remind us of a different place from the place where we live. Perhaps children have collected pebbles or shells from the beach. Explain that the souvenir brought back by Dan and Mary had been bought in a shop, and was arranged with shells to support it on a little platform ('mounted on a cockleshell pedestal'). It was known as the Gift because it was a present for the children's mother.

◆ Establish that the Gift had been kept on the mantelpiece (a shelf over the fireplace). Ask the children whether they think this might have had anything to do with the hatching. Perhaps the warmth of the fire had helped the creature to develop inside the egg.

◆ Discuss the family's reaction to the appearance of the creature. Was everyone friendly towards it? How did the creature feel? (Frightened at first, but soon won over by the friendliness.)

◆ Talk about what the creature might be. Do the children think it is a real animal or a made-up creature? Why do the children think Mrs Kane called it a 'lamb'?

Vocabulary

Living, not living, eggs, hatch, care, food, water, shelter, differences.

Science activities

◆ Provide some hen's eggs and egg-shaped pebbles for the children to examine. They can compare their shape, colour and weight, how they feel in the hand, and how strong they think they are. Record the children's comments on a flip chart, using different-coloured pens to highlight similarities and differences.

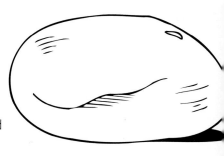

◆ Talk about the major difference between a stone and an egg: a stone is not alive but an egg is (if fresh). A stone can never move or change of its own accord, while an egg could develop and hatch into a new creature (if given the right conditions). An egg could also provide food for another animal, whereas a stone cannot. The children can write some points of information to help them distinguish between a pebble and an egg.

◆ Ask the children to draw, and write sentences about, other creatures (as many as they can) that hatch from a shelled egg. They will know about birds, and can perhaps find out about turtles and snakes. Take this opportunity to tell the children that they should avoid disturbing birds in the wild, and should never remove eggs from nests.

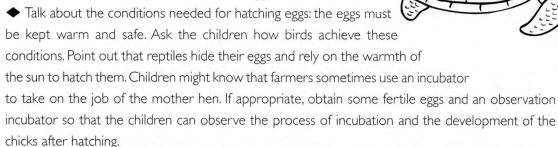

◆ Talk about the conditions needed for hatching eggs: the eggs must be kept warm and safe. Ask the children how birds achieve these conditions. Point out that reptiles hide their eggs and rely on the warmth of the sun to hatch them. Children might know that farmers sometimes use an incubator to take on the job of the mother hen. If appropriate, obtain some fertile eggs and an observation incubator so that the children can observe the process of incubation and the development of the chicks after hatching.

◆ Remind the children about looking after animals in our care. Make a list of their needs, including: the correct type of food, fresh water, a quiet place to sleep with suitable bedding, careful handling and treatment when ill. The children can design a poster for a pet shop or vet's surgery, reminding people how to look after their pets.

Further literacy ideas

◆ Look closely at the first sentence and talk about how the author, Helen Cresswell, tells us what has happened in a few words: the Gift has appeared and then disappeared – it came 'like a shooting star, brushed their lives with magic, and vanished'. By the time this passage starts, the Gift has already gone; so what follows is a retelling.

◆ If the children have not seen an artist's interpretation of the Gift, encourage them to describe what they think hatched from the egg. They can draw and label the creature, seeking out clues in the text: the animal was odd, sleek and grey, and was small enough to sit on the mantelpiece.

◆ Encourage the children to take part in reading out the conversation. They can underline the spoken words, using different colours for Mary, Mrs Kane, Dan and Mr Kane.

◆ Identify the verbs relating to the actions of the Gift: come, brushed, vanished, hatched, scooted and peered. With the help of the text, the children can write a new sentence using each of these words in a new context.

◆ Give the children a photocopied sketch of the outline of a fireplace with a mantelpiece; ask them to complete the picture by adding the fire, the clock, the green glass cat and the egg before it hatched.

Genre
story
(retelling of events)

The Gift grows

The Gift had made short work of anything in sight. Fish, chips, biscuits, buckets of scraps. Every day he seemed to double in size. By the time Dan and Mary entered him for the Pet Show he had to be pushed there in a wheelbarrow. (He won a Special Prize, as Most Unusual Pet.)

It was all very well, as Mr Kane pointed out, to have a hamster as a pet, or a goldfish, a cat, a parrot, a dog – even a big dog, like an Irish Wolfhound. But at the rate the Gift was going, he would have eaten them out of house and home.

'If you ask me,' Uncle Fred had said, 'it's a sort of Loch Ness Monster you've got there.'

He had even wondered whether the Gift might end up polishing off human beings for breakfast, dinner and tea.

The Gift grows

This text continues the story of the Gift, describing how the creature has grown.

Display pictures of strange creatures that may or may not exist, such as the Loch Ness Monster. Collect pictures of young and adult animals, including ones (such as frogs and butterflies) that have a larval stage.

Science learning objectives

◆ To know that animals, including humans, move, feed, grow, use their senses and reproduce (Sc2 1b).

◆ To know that humans and other animals need food and water to stay alive (Sc2 2b).

◆ To know that eating the right types and amounts of food helps humans to stay healthy (Sc2 2c).

◆ To know how to treat animals with care and sensitivity (Sc2 2e).

◆ To know that humans and other animals can produce offspring and that these offspring grow into adults (Sc2 2f).

Discussing the text

◆ Ask the children whether they can remember why the creature is called the Gift and why the word is always given a capital letter. They should recall that the Kane children always referred to the present they had brought back for their mother as the Gift from Winklesea – so when a strange creature hatched out, if became known as the Gift.

◆ Look at some of the phrases used in the text and find out whether the children understand their meaning: *short work, double in size, house and home, polishing off.* Ask children to invent new sentences, in other contexts, that use these phrases.

◆ Can the children explain why Mr Kane and Uncle Fred were worried about the new pet?

Vocabulary

Animals, healthy, food, care, change, grow.

Science activities

◆ The children will know that all young animals need food to grow. Make a list of foods the children like to eat. Group these into foods they eat very often, fairly often and occasionally. Talk about these groups, and emphasize the need to eat a range of different foods in order to be healthy. Make a large chart with simple drawings of familiar foods. Ask the children to select one day's food for themselves or a friend, making sure that the meals they provide are healthy. (Be aware of cultural and family circumstances.)

◆ Discuss the eating habits of pets. Ask the children to help you make a list of foods that pets are likely to eat, such as cereals, leaves, carrots, meat, bones, bread, grain, seeds and (of course) water. Use this information to make a chart on which the children can record the food requirements of their pets (see illustration below).

◆ Remind the children that all animals change as they grow older. Provide pictures of young and adult animals for matching. Ask the children to describe changes that have happened to themselves since they were born. Perhaps they can predict further changes that will take place before they become adults.

Food for pets

	dog	cat	rabbit	hamster	mouse
cereals	✔		✔	✔	✔
leaves			✔		
carrots			✔	✔	✔
meat	✔	✔			
bones	✔	✔			
bread					✔
biscuits	✔				
grain				✔	✔
seeds			✔	✔	✔
water	✔	✔	✔	✔	✔

Further literacy ideas

◆ Collect uses of the word 'double' that the children have come across, such as 'double six' on dice, 'double your money', 'double trouble' or a person's 'double' (meaning twin or lookalike).

◆ Write a class story about something growing too big: either an animal or a plant (for example, a beanstalk).

◆ Organize a 'Show for Unusual Pets'. Each child can draw and describe his or her own strange imaginary pet, explaining what it likes to eat and where it lives. Create a class story about what happened at the show.

Genre
information
leaflet/
advertisement

WHITE POST MODERN FARM CENTRE

Visit our award-winning farm in winter and you'll still be sure of a warm welcome. You'll always find plenty to do – both indoors and out!

- See our special Nativity Play in a stable with real animals, and even take part!
- Visit our Christmas Shop selling unusual gifts and decorations.
- Wander among the delightful hand-painted scenery.
- Look inside the Elves' Cottage.
- Free children's gift from Santa.
- Free mince pie for the grown-ups.
- Every day from mid-November until Christmas Eve.

Indoor attractions
- Incubator Room
- Mouse Town
- Angora Rabbit Shed
- Night-Time Owl Walk
- Reptile House
- Green Farm Barn
- Silver Barn (larger animals)
- Pig House
- Pet Centre
- Always baby animals to hold!

Winter at the White Post Farm

This leaflet describes the attractions and activities that people will enjoy if they visit this farm. It is both information text and advertisement.

Display pictures of familiar farm animals and their young, as well as other animals mentioned in the leaflet: owls, rabbits, mice and reptiles.

Science learning objectives

◆ To know that animals need food and water to stay alive (Sc2 2b).

◆ To know how to treat animals with care and sensitivity (Sc2 2e).

◆ To know that animals can produce offspring and that these offspring grow into adults (Sc2 2f).

◆ To group living things according to observable similarities and differences (Sc2 4b).

◆ To recognize that there are hazards in living things (Breadth of study 2b).

Discussing the text

◆ Explain that the text is part of a leaflet inviting people to visit a farm centre. Ask the children what clues they can spot that indicate the time of year. (The word 'winter', the snow on the title, the mention of Christmas.)

◆ Discuss the children's preferences: which attractions would they choose to see first?

◆ Talk about how the attractions are described, and how the information is arranged in lists with a spot or bullet for each item. Is there a reason for this? (It separates them, makes them stand out and so makes them easier to read.)

◆ What do the children think of a nativity play with real animals? Would they enjoy it? Would there be any problems? Would the animals involved enjoy it? Would it be a good idea to have real animals in a concert at school?

◆ Does the information given in the leaflet persuade the children that they would like to visit the farm centre? Explain that visitors have to pay, and ask what the money is used for. (To buy food for the animals; to pay for their homes and bedding, and for the vet if they become ill: to pay the wages of the staff who are needed to care for the animals.)

Vocabulary

Animals, farm, care, caring, shelter, food, water, birds, incubator.

Science activities

◆ Make a list of animals the children would expect to see on a farm. Divide the list into two groups, mammals and birds – for example: cattle, pigs, sheep, goats and horses in one group and hens, ducks and turkeys in the other. Ask the children to find differences between the two groups.

◆ Talk about the other animals that can be seen at the farm centre: rabbits, mice, owls and reptiles. Find out whether anyone knows the names of any reptiles (snakes, lizards, turtles and tortoises). Encourage the children to try and place these animals in the previous groups. Perhaps they will suggest giving the reptiles a group of their own.

◆ What would the children expect to see in the incubator room? Explain that an incubator takes the place of a mother bird, such as a hen or duck: it provides the warmth needed for the eggs to develop and the baby birds to hatch out. If appropriate, obtain an observation incubator and some fertile eggs for the children to look after in the classroom.

◆ Talk about the responsibility of caring for animals, including pets. Ask the children to draw a particular animal (such as a sheep or a horse) and write down its requirements: type of food, fresh water daily, suitable shelter and bedding, careful handling. Emphasize the need to wash your hands after touching any animal, because of the possibility of spreading disease.

◆ Talk about the stages in the lives of familiar animals: babies grow into adults, then have young of their own. Discuss the numbers of young born to a mother at one time: usually one calf, but a litter of kittens and a brood of chicks. The children can work in groups to make a poster showing mother animals and their babies: a cow with a calf, a pig with some piglets, a duck with some ducklings and so on.

Further literacy ideas

◆ Encourage the children to look again at how the leaflet is set out. What do they think are the advantages of making a list, instead of writing full sentences, when creating a leaflet? (People can find the information quickly; there is more space on the leaflet for pictures and photographs.) Ask them to choose one attraction involving animals and write a more detailed description of what people might expect to see.

◆ Identify words that instruct people: *visit, see, wander, look inside*. Help the children to understand why this is a successful method of telling people what is available. Do they think it sounds bossy? Ask them to write some points for a leaflet that will make people want to visit the school at Christmas – for example: *See our wonderful Christmas tree. Enjoy the mince pies Class 2 have baked. Wander around our brilliantly decorated classroom. Look at Bronwen's picture of the three wise men. See Dean's amazing calendar.*

◆ Organize a survey of the top attractions at White Post Farm. The children can each say (or write down) which three things they would most like to see. Present the results as a graph, so that the children can discover which attractions would be the most popular. Where would the queues be?

Genre
story poem

Hiawatha's childhood

By the shores of Gitche Gumee,
By the shining Big-Sea-Water,
Stood the wigwam of Nokomis,
Daughter of the Moon, Nokomis.
Dark behind it rose the forest,
Rose the black and gloomy pine-trees.
    There the wrinkled, old Nokomis
Nursed the little Hiawatha,
Rocked him in his linden cradle,
Bedded soft in moss and rushes.
    At the door on Summer evenings
Sat the little Hiawatha;
Heard the whispering of pine-trees,
Heard the lapping of the water,
Sounds of music, words of wonder;
'Minne-wawa!' said the pine-trees,
'Mudway-aushka!' said the water.

(from **The Story of Hiawatha** by HW Longfellow)

Hiawatha's childhood

Explain that Hiawatha lived in the forests of North America many years ago, and that his life would be very different from that of a child reading about him today. Collect pictures and books about babies and children in different times and cultures, and about the native American way of life.

This part of the poem by HW Longfellow describes how Hiawatha was cared for as a baby in the forest.

Science learning objectives

◆ To know that humans and other animals can produce offspring and that these offspring grow into adults (Sc2 2f).

◆ To know about the senses that enable humans and other animals to be aware of the world around them (Sc2 2g).

◆ To identify different light sources, including the Sun (Sc4 3a).

◆ To know that darkness is the absence of light (Sc4 3b).

◆ To know that there are many kinds of sound and sources of sound (Sc4 3c).

Discussing the text

◆ Allow the children to enjoy the rhythm, sounds and atmosphere of the poem, rather than trying to understand every word. Encourage them to repeat the strange words together, enjoying the sounds of *Hiawatha, Gitche Gumee, Nokomis* and *Big-Sea-Water*.

◆ Make sure the children understand that Nokomis is caring for the baby Hiawatha, and that their home is a tent made of animal skins called a *wigwam*. Discuss the scene with the children, so that they can imagine what Hiawatha would see from the wigwam. Compare the shining lake known as Big-Sea-Water and the dark forest of pine trees.

◆ Talk about the cradle where the baby would spend much of his time. Explain that linden is a type of wood, and the moss and rushes would be gathered from around the lake to make the baby comfortable.

◆ Emphasize the sounds of the scene. Encourage the children to practise making the whispering of the pine trees by repeating 'Minne-wawa!' and the lapping of the water by chanting 'Mudway-aushka!'

Vocabulary

Baby, nursed, cradle, senses, eyes, see, sight, dark, light, bright, ears, hear, heard, listening, sounds.

Science activities

◆ Encourage the children to compare Hiawatha's babyhood with their own. First establish what is similar: an adult needs to take care of the baby, which cannot move about to find food or keep itself clean; the baby needs a safe place to sleep and a home for shelter. Then look for differences in the type of home and the material used for bedding. The children can use drawings and sentences to record the differences between the wigwam and their own home, and between the wooden cradle and a modern cot.

◆ Move on to thinking about toys and transport. What would Hiawatha have played with? How would Nokomis have moved him from place to place? Compare the answers with the children's own experiences.

◆ Discuss how the baby Hiawatha, as he grew, would use his senses to discover the world he was living in.

He would notice the brightness of the water and the darkness of the forest as he used his sense of sight. Ask the children to look towards the brightest part of the room, perhaps the window or a bright light (but not the Sun – warn them never to look directly at this), and then to find the darkest area in the room. By listening, Hiawatha would identify the different sounds around him and know which was the lapping water, the whispering trees and so on. By closing their eyes and listening carefully, the children can find out which sounds they can recognize. List these and compare them with sounds the children can identify when out of doors. Ask which are the loudest and the softest sounds. Are there any unpleasant sounds? Are there any 'sounds of music, words of wonder' in their environment? (Distinguish between naturally 'musical' sounds, such as birdsong, and those made using instruments.) Which is the children's favourite sound?

Further literacy ideas

◆ Turn the poem into a sound performance. Groups of children can practise making the sounds of the water and the pine trees. Others can join in to recite the lines, perhaps acting the parts of Nokomis and Hiawatha.

◆ Talk about Nokomis. What might she look like? What kind of person was she? Use books and pictures to help the children imagine the native American way of life.

◆ Make a frieze depicting the forest scene. Show the contrast of bright and dark. The children could write sentences to tell the story and explain the experiences of Hiawatha as a child; the sentences can be arranged around the collage.

Hiawatha and the animals

Genre
story poem

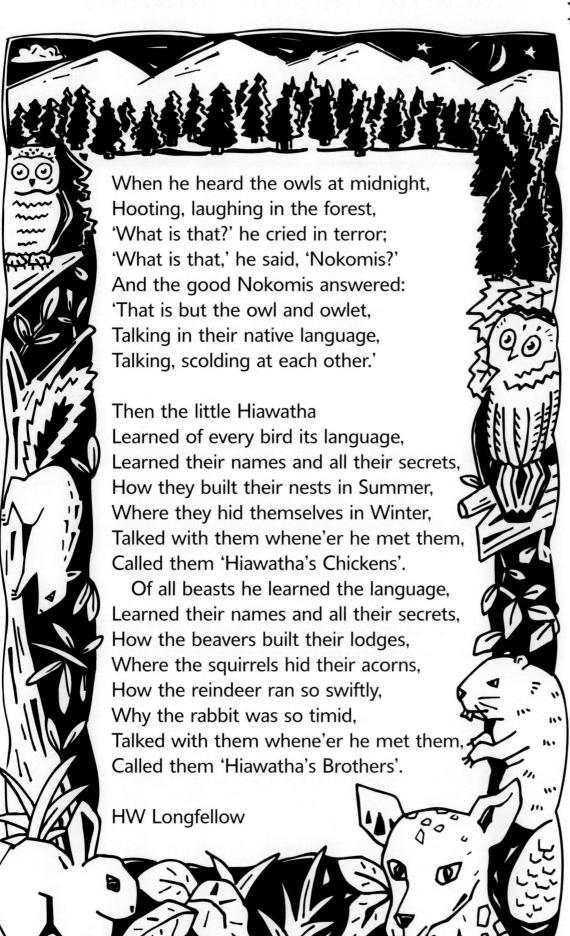

When he heard the owls at midnight,
Hooting, laughing in the forest,
'What is that?' he cried in terror;
'What is that,' he said, 'Nokomis?'
And the good Nokomis answered:
'That is but the owl and owlet,
Talking in their native language,
Talking, scolding at each other.'

Then the little Hiawatha
Learned of every bird its language,
Learned their names and all their secrets,
How they built their nests in Summer,
Where they hid themselves in Winter,
Talked with them whene'er he met them,
Called them 'Hiawatha's Chickens'.
   Of all beasts he learned the language,
Learned their names and all their secrets,
How the beavers built their lodges,
Where the squirrels hid their acorns,
How the reindeer ran so swiftly,
Why the rabbit was so timid,
Talked with them whene'er he met them,
Called them 'Hiawatha's Brothers'.

HW Longfellow

Hiawatha and the animals

This part of the poem by H W Longfellow describes the young Hiawatha discovering the world around him.

Remind the children that Hiawatha grew up in a forest on the edge of a lake, and that he soon learned to recognize familiar sights and sounds. Before reading the new text, ask the children whether they can remember any of these. Obtain pictures of the animals mentioned in the text.

Science learning objectives

◆ To make and record observations (Sc1 2f).

◆ To compare findings with what was predicted, and try to explain them, drawing on knowledge and understanding (Sc1 2i).

◆ To know about the senses that enable humans and other animals to be aware of the world around them (Sc2 2g).

◆ To find out about the different kinds of animals in the local environment (Sc2 5a).

◆ To identify similarities and differences between local environments and ways in which these affect animals and plants that are found there (Sc2 5b).

Discussing the text

◆ Ask the children to help you underline or make a list of the names of the creatures mentioned in the text. Explain that people sometimes use the word 'beasts' for animals, especially larger animals with fur. Display pictures of these animals.

◆ Talk about the sounds of the owls. Do the children think Hiawatha was still afraid when he knew what the hooting was? Relate this to any experiences the children may have of unknown sounds in the night.

◆ Can the children think why Hiawatha was such an expert on the forest animals when he was so young? (They were all around him and he saw them every day, watched them carefully and did not frighten them away.)

◆ Ask the children whether they can recognize the 'language' of any birds. They might mention the chirping of sparrows, a robin singing, a cuckoo, a crow or an owl.

◆ Talk about the 'language' of the beasts. Can the children imitate the voices of any animals?

◆ Why do the children think Hiawatha called the birds his 'Chickens' and the beasts his 'Brothers'?

Vocabulary

Animals, creatures, beasts, birds, grow, senses, sight, sound, hear, listen, habitat.

Science activities

◆ Explain that all animals can be put into groups, according to what they look like. Ask the children to make two lists of animals they know: one of birds and one of furry animals (mammals). Talk about how they will decide which animals to put in each group: birds have beaks, two legs and feathers, and are usually able to fly; mammals have four legs and a covering of hair (which may be spiky, as in a hedgehog).

◆ Ask the children which senses they would use to recognize these animals in the wild. Which animals would they see? Which would they hear?

◆ Use illustrations of the animals mentioned in the poem to build up a picture of the pine forest environment; alternatively, they could be added to the frieze made in the previous activity (see page 58). Discuss how each creature finds a suitable home (or habitat) in the forest. The birds have plenty of nesting places, and can eat insects and berries on the trees. Beavers need wood to gnaw to make their lodges (homes) and water in which to catch fish. Squirrels need trees for nesting and nuts to gather, store and eat. Reindeer need places to hide from their enemies and leaves to nibble. Rabbits will eat the grass around the trees and lake, and dig burrows in the soil.

◆ Choose a familiar habitat for the children to investigate – perhaps a single tree, an overgrown grassy area or a patch of shrubs. Encourage them to observe carefully and make a record of all the animals found there. The observations can take place during a single session, or for a few minutes each day. Close observation will reveal small creatures such as woodlice, ladybirds, snails and beetles; quiet, more distant observation is necessary to see any birds. Perhaps the children will suggest why larger animals such as a fox, hedgehog or wood mouse will probably not be seen: there are too many people about; there are not enough places for them to hide.

◆ Find two contrasting habitats for the children to compare, perhaps an area of mown grass and an area of overgrown ground, or a pot plant and a plant growing in the garden. Ask them to predict what animals they may find in each habitat; encourage them to explain any differences they discover.

Further literacy ideas

◆ Ask the children to describe Hiawatha as a child. Help them to build up a picture of a curious, quiet boy who notices things, listens carefully and understands the ways of animals.

◆ Ask the children to look closely at the words that tell you more about the animals. Write words out for the children to match: *beaver, squirrel, reindeer, rabbit, built, hid, ran, was, lodges, acorns, swiftly, timid.*

◆ Point out that the animals the poet writes about have two syllables to their names: *rab-bit, bea-ver, squir-rel, rein-deer.* What other animals do they know with names like that? Make a list of animals with one-syllable names, such as *pig, dog* and *cat.*

◆ Collect words in both texts that describe sounds: *talking, scolding, hooting, laughing, whispering, lapping.* Add these to the forest collage. Can the children think of words to describe the everyday sounds they hear?

Genre
instructions

How you can help your doctor

1. Always carry a handkerchief. Use it to blow your nose or cover your face if you sneeze.

2. Put your hand over your mouth when you cough.

3. Always wash your hands when you have been to the toilet.

4. Wash cuts and grazes and cover them with a plaster or bandage.

5. Keep away from fires and cookers.

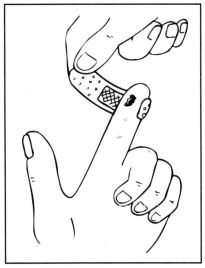

6. Don't touch electric sockets.

In an emergency, dial **999** to call an ambulance. Tell the operator your name and address.

How you can help your doctor

Display pictures and books relating to how people can keep healthy and safe.

This text encourages children to consider their health and well-being.

Science learning objectives
◆ Learn about the role of drugs as medicines (Sc2 2d).
◆ Learn about everyday appliances that use electricity (Sc4 1a).
◆ Recognize that there are hazards in living things, materials and physical processes, and assess risks and take action to reduce risks to themselves and others (Breadth of study 2b).

Discussing the text
◆ Refer to the numbers of the points listed when discussing the text, so that the children begin to understand the purpose of arranging information in this way.
◆ Ask why it is important to use a handkerchief when you cough and sneeze. Make sure the children understand how easily germs are spread. Explain that germs are very small living things that are all around us, but which we cannot see; they are often responsible for making us ill.
◆ Refer to point 3 and explain how germs on hands are spread by touching books, furniture and food.
◆ Talk about why cuts and grazes need to be kept clean: because germs in dirt can get into the blood and cause infections.
◆ Can the children explain in what way points 5 and 6 are different from the first four? (Points 1-4 are concerned with the activity of germs, points 5 and 6 with non-biological hazards).
◆ Talk about what an 'emergency' is. Explain that most of the time, a parent or carer will know whether to phone for an ambulance. Emphasize that it is very unlikely that a young child will need to dial 999 – but is important that they know what to do if necessary. Point out that unnecessary calls waste ambulance time, and so put other people at risk.

Vocabulary
Doctor, healthy, unhealthy, germs, medicines, danger, safe.

Science activities
◆ Identify parts of the body that are likely to carry germs when you have a cough, a cold or 'flu: the nose, mouth, throat and hands. Explain that we cannot avoid all germs, but can become really ill if we catch certain types.
◆ Emphasize the importance of always washing hands after visiting the toilet and before handling food. Talk about how every person plays a part in preventing the spread of disease.
◆ Take this opportunity to emphasize the safe use of medicines. Tell the children that sometimes, when we are ill, we need to take medicines. Explain that medicines can be dangerous, and must only be taken by children when a doctor or parent decides it is necessary. Encourage questions about the use, packaging and safe keeping of medicines. Ask the children to write a set of instructions for taking medicines, including: keeping them out of the reach of small children; only keeping them in the correct packaging; only taking them with a parent's consent; always taking the right amount (too

much of a medicine can be very dangerous).

◆ Talk about sources of heat that the children are likely to come into contact with, and the need to take care to avoid getting burnt or scalded. Refer to cookers, hot kettles, heaters, hot water, bonfires, fireworks and the strength of the Sun in summer. Explain that human skin is easily burned and takes a long time to heal.

◆ Remind the children about electrical safety: mains electricity can kill; plugs, cables and sockets should always be kept clean and dry; sockets should never be touched.

Further literacy ideas

◆ Highlight significant 'health words' words in the text such as *sneeze, cough, wash, hands, face, nose, grazes, plaster* and *bandage*. Use them in a Dictionary of Health.

◆ Ask the children to make their own list of numbered instructions. Perhaps they could tell others how to help their dentist (cleaning teeth properly, not eating very sugary foods, going for regular checkups) or help at home (putting toys away, packing a schoolbag, finding clothes and so on).

◆ Help the children to turn the statements in the text into questions – for example: *What should you do if you sneeze? When should you wash your hands?* Have an oral question and answer session, or write the questions and answers on cards for the children to match.

Riddles: All about us

Genre
riddles

We have an important job to do.
So we need cleaning every day.
We help you enjoy your food.
What are we?

You visit me when you are hurt or feeling ill.
I might look in your mouth, or listen to your chest.
Sometimes I give you medicine.
Who am I?

Sleeping all day long,
Needing lots of care and help.
Making very funny noises
And only drinking milk.
What can it be?

What is bright and colourful,
Orange or red, perhaps green, purple or yellow,
Grows on trees
And you should eat some every day?

My eyes tell me it is bright and beautiful.
My fingers tell me it is soft and smooth.
My nose tells me how lovely its scent is.
My ears tell me it is very quiet.
But I must leave its taste to the bumblebee!
What could it be?

Riddles: All about us

These riddles introduce children to word puzzles, and encourage them to look for clues to the answers.

Present the riddles one at a time, letting the children focus their attention on each.

Science learning objectives

◆ To be aware of human beings as animals, including knowledge of their body parts, dietary and health needs, reproduction and senses (Sc2 1b, 2a-d, 2f, 2g).

◆ To use simple scientific language to communicate ideas and to name and describe living things (Breadth of study 2a).

Discussing the text

◆ Choose an appropriate riddle to read to the children - perhaps as an introduction to a science topic, in relation to current science work or as revision. At this stage, keep out of sight any pictures or specimens to be used with later discussion.

◆ Consider all suggestions made by the children, avoiding too much early emphasis on finding the 'right' answer. Value all suggestions, even when they will eventually be judged inappropriate. Use words such as 'could be' and 'not really' rather than outright negatives.

◆ Encourage the children to give their answer as a simple sentence appropriate to the question, rather than a single word.

◆ Focus on the need for a question mark at the end of each riddle; point out that this means an answer is required.

◆ Explain that **all** the clues in each riddle should be considered to arrive at an answer.

Riddle 1 Answer: You are our teeth.

◆ Remind the children that this riddle relates to themselves; if necessary, give clues to indicate that the answer is a part of their body.

◆ Ask the children how they know that the riddle refers to several teeth, not just to one.

Riddle 2 Answer: You are my doctor.

◆ This riddle gives the children an opportunity to share their experiences of visiting a doctor.

Riddle 3 Answer: It could be a new-born baby or a new-born kitten or puppy.

◆ Encourage the children to suggest a range of possibilities. Discuss which clues might describe themselves (as children) and which indicate that the answer must be a new-born animal.

Riddle 4 Answer: It must be all kinds of fruit.

◆ You may prefer to read the lines one at a time, asking for suggestions which fit the clues. Make sure the children understand that every suggestion which fits a clue is appropriate until it is eliminated by a further clue.

◆ Talk about the word *fruit* as referring to a group of things that are similar.

◆ Ask the children to think of fruits that are the colours described in the riddle.

Riddle 5 Answer: It could be any kind of flower.

◆ As you read the riddle, emphasize the senses described by pointing to your eyes, nose and ears and wiggling your fingers and tongue; encourage the children to do the same.

◆ Ask the children which clue they think is the most important in helping them guess the answer. Which clues make them think of other things such as a toy, some scented soap or a piece of fabric?

◆ Use this opportunity to explain that some flowers could be harmful if tasted, and that nothing should be picked and eaten without an adult's permission.

Vocabulary

Teeth, doctor, medicines, baby, fruit, flower, clues, questions, answers.

Science activities

Riddle 1

◆ Talk about the importance of teeth, and which foods we would have difficulty eating if we did not have any teeth.

◆ Remind the children that it is essential for them to keep their teeth clean and make regular visits to the dentist.

Riddle 2

◆ Talk about the medicines we sometimes need to make us better when we are ill.

◆ Encourage the children to ask questions about doctors, medicines and health.

◆ Take this opportunity to help the children distinguish clearly between medicines and sweets. Identify the packaging used for medicines, and talk about the proper use of all medicines.

Riddle 3

◆ Children with new brothers and sisters can be consulted about the accuracy of the information given in this riddle. Discuss what other creatures the clues might fit, such as kittens, puppies and baby mice. What babies do not behave in this way? (For example, calves and lambs are active soon after birth; baby birds need help from their parents, but do not drink milk.)

Riddle 4

◆ Display pictures and specimens of a range of fruits. Remind the children that all fruits come from plants, and many from trees. Discuss how they could be grouped (perhaps according to colour).

◆ Emphasize the importance of fruit as part of our daily diet. Discuss what people mean when they say 'An apple a day keeps the doctor away.'

◆ You could organize a tasting session - but be sure to maintain thorough hygiene conditions and be aware of food allergies. Warn the children that some fruits they see on trees are poisonous and should not be sampled.

Riddle 5

◆ Remind the children how they use their five senses to investigate the world around them.

◆ Provide different flowers for the children to investigate by looking, touching and smelling.

◆ Ask the children to draw a diagram, using arrows, symbols and words, to show how they use their different senses to find out about a flower.

◆ Talk about the bumblebee tasting the flower as it gathers pollen and nectar. Which other senses do the children think the bee uses to find the flower?

Further literacy ideas

Riddle 1

◆ Ask the children to extend the riddle by providing another clue suitable for teeth, perhaps referring to their shape and colour.

◆ Encourage the children to make up their own riddle about their ears, nose, tongue or hands.

Riddle 2

◆ Use this riddle as a model for class riddles about other people connected with keeping healthy, such as a dentist, optician or school cook.

Riddle 3

◆ The children can create riddles to describe themselves. These can be read out anonymously for the rest of the class to solve.

◆ Riddles can be created to describe other stages in life, such as a toddler, parent or grandparent.

Riddle 4

◆ The children can make up their own riddles to describe a specific fruit or a different type of food. Ask them to draw a picture of the food separately, so that others can match the riddle with the picture.

Riddle 5

◆ Provide objects such as a sponge, a tambourine, a bar of soap, scented paper and a metal lid, so that the children can investigate with appropriate senses (seeing, touching and listening) and compose their own riddles (using the original riddle as a model).

Create a class book of riddles, with the answers (as words or an illustration) hidden under a flaps at the foot of the page.

Riddles: Animals

Genre
riddles

I like to eat slugs.
I live in a pond.
I am good at jumping.
What am I?

I like to be out in the dark.
I fly very quietly with my feathery wings.
I swallow my food whole.
What am I?

I'm made of twigs and grass and moss,
Well-hidden in a hedge.
I hold babies safely when they hatch,
Until they are strong enough to fly away.
What am I?

If you find me living under a stone,
Hiding from the wind and sun,
Leave me to enjoy the dark and damp.
I'll creep out when it's night-time and you've gone.
What could I be?

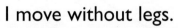

I move without legs.
I swim but cannot walk.
I dive but cannot fly.
I travel hundreds of miles.
Of course I'm much bigger than you.
What am I?

Riddles: Animals

These riddles introduce children to word puzzles, and encourage them to look for clues to the answers.

Present the riddles one at a time, letting the children focus their attention on each.

Science learning objectives

◆ To be aware of the external features, life processes, needs and environment of a range of animals (Sc2 1b, c; 2a, b, e, f, g; 5a).

◆ To use simple scientific language to communicate ideas and to name and describe living things (Breadth of study 2a).

Discussing the text

◆ With each riddle, focus on use of a question mark at the end and explain that an answer is required. Encourage the children to give their answer as a sentence, rather than a single word.

◆ Explain that **all** the clues in each riddle should be considered to arrive at an answer.

◆ Read the first riddle and ask the children to provide an answer. They should recognize that the clues describe a frog. Explain that the correct answer to the question 'What am I?' is 'You are a frog'. Ask whether the children think there was one clue that really gave away the answer.

◆ Read the second riddle one line at a time, covering the remaining lines so that the children have the opportunity to think and consider all the possibilities. Say that this riddle also describes a creature they will have heard of. After the first line, ask for ideas. What creatures like to be out in the dark? Make a list of suggestions, such as a hedgehog, bat, fox, moth, owl, badger, cat and so on. Reveal the second line and eliminate ideas that no longer fit the description. Then see whether the next clue confirms any of the remaining suggestions. Encourage the children to give the complete answer: 'You are an owl.'

◆ Read the third riddle slowly, giving the children time to think about the clues. If necessary, help them by asking: *What kind of babies hatch? What creatures will fly away?* Read the riddle again, so that the children can reply together: 'You are a bird's nest.'

◆ The clues of the fourth riddle fit a number of creatures, such as a woodlouse, slug, beetle, centipede, earthworm or perhaps toad. Make a list of all suggestions; remind the children that the animals must be quite small and prefer to be where it is dark and damp, out of the way of bigger animals such as humans.

◆ Read the last riddle one line at a time. After the first line, ask the children which creatures move around without the help of legs. Make a list of suggested creatures. After the second line is revealed, eliminate any that cannot swim and discuss the remaining animals. Follow the same pattern after the next line. With the next clue, talk about distances: the creature must live in the sea or a big river, not in a pond or stream. From the last clue, the children should decide that the creature is a whale (or perhaps a shark) and not a small fish.

Vocabulary

Animal, creature, habitat, home, question, answer, clue.

Science activities

Riddle 1

◆ Ask the children to draw a picture of a jumping frog by a pond, looking for slugs. They could write the riddle in a speech bubble. Talk about the usefulness of frogs in gardens: they help us by eating slugs, which damage crops such as strawberries and lettuces. If appropriate, visit a pond to investigate the creatures living there. Explain that we can only observe frogs if we are quiet and that these creatures must always be left undisturbed in their natural habitat.

Riddle 2

◆ Provide pictures of owls and their prey. Talk about the features of this bird that make it a good hunter: its ability to remain still; its silent wings, hooked beak and grasping claws. Consider the importance of being able to see in poor light. Create a night-time scene, perhaps set in the immediate environment, showing a range of creatures that might appear during the hours of darkness.

Riddle 3

◆ Talk about the stages in the life cycle of birds. Do the children know of other places where birds might build nests, other than in hedgerows? Remind them never to disturb nesting birds: explain that if animals are unable to complete their life cycles, there will be no further families.

Riddle 4

◆ With the children's help, arrange some stones and pieces of wood in an undisturbed part of the school grounds. After a week, investigate the new habitats and record any inhabitants. Make sure that the children treat the animals and their homes with respect. Ask the children to draw some of the creatures discovered; use their drawings to make a display. Ask them to write an advertisement for the new homes: *ideal for dark-loving families, plenty of cracks and holes for hiding, always damp, little disturbance* and so on.

Riddle 5

◆ Using pictures and children's drawings of a range of animals, ask the children to sort the animals according to how they move - for example, animals that can fly, swim or walk. Identify creatures that use more than one method to travel. Ask the children to describe the movements of a duck.

Further literacy ideas

Riddles 1 and 2

◆ Use these as models for class riddles about other animals. The children can progress to writing their own riddles, with the answers as separate illustrations for matching or hidden under a flap at the bottom of the page.

◆ Focus on the vocabulary for phonic and spelling practice. Ask the children to identify 'g' sounds in the first riddle and 'f' sounds in the second.

Riddle 3

◆ Compose riddles about other homes or habitats, such as: in a pond, in a tree, under the ground, under a stone.

◆ Ask the children to think of other words beginning with *tw, gr* and *fl*.

◆ Point out the plural form of *baby*.

Riddle 4

◆ Suggest that the children write extra clues, so that the answer to this riddle is a specific creature. Other lines could describe a woodlouse, beetle or earthworm.

◆ Find words that are the opposite of *dark, damp, under, enjoy, night*.

Riddle 5

◆ Make a list of all kinds of movement that animals use to travel, including *swim, fly, crawl, slither* and so on. Encourage the children to copy some of these movements safely in a PE session.

Plants

Plants are very important. They were the first living things on the Earth. Animals depend on them for their existence. Humans rely on plants as a source of food; to feed their animals; to provide shelter and fuel; to provide materials for clothing and other everyday articles; and as a source of medicines.

From an early age, children need to recognize and appreciate the importance of plants. They should begin to understand something of the relationship between plants and animals (including themselves), particularly in relation to their immediate environment.

The texts in this chapter introduce children to a range of plants, demonstrating the wide variety within the plant kingdom: from mighty trees to the humble dandelion; from the familiar plants encountered every day to exotic specimens which need special care to be grown by us. The texts emphasize the vulnerability of plants, as well as their ability to survive.

The texts can be used to demonstrate the different parts of plants, the stages of a plant's life cycle and the conditions needed for a plant to grow well. The children will begin to understand the importance of seeds in the life of a plant: seeds are essential for the continuing existence of flowering plants. Some texts emphasize our need to ensure that plants grow well, so that we are provided with food.

The children are encouraged to take notice of plants around them, to observe the details of their lives more carefully, and to develop a sensitive attitude towards plants. As well as stressing the usefulness of plants, the texts warn of the hazards that are associated with some plants.

The texts provide valuable opportunities for first-hand experience and development of investigative skills. The children are expected to observe the development of plants and record this through writing, drawing and photography. They are encouraged to sow seeds and tend for growing plants, enjoying the responsibility of helping to look after a fragile seedling or a strong tree.

It is important to excite a child's curiosity about plants at an early age, thus stimulating a lifelong understanding of the importance of plants and their place within the environment. With this enthusiasm, the children will gain results that stimulate continued interest – whether through following a career in studying, growing or using plants, or in tending a flower garden and growing food for the family.

Trees

Trees are the kindest things I know,
They do no harm, they simply grow

And spread a shade for sleepy cows,
And gather birds among their boughs.

They give us fruit in leaves above,
And wood to make our houses of,

And leaves to burn on Hallowe'en
And in the Spring new buds of green.

They are the first when day's begun
To touch the beams of morning sun,

They are the last to hold the light
When evening changes into night,

And when a moon floats on the sky
They hum a drowsy lullaby

Of sleepy children long ago...
Trees are the kindest things I know.

Harry Behn

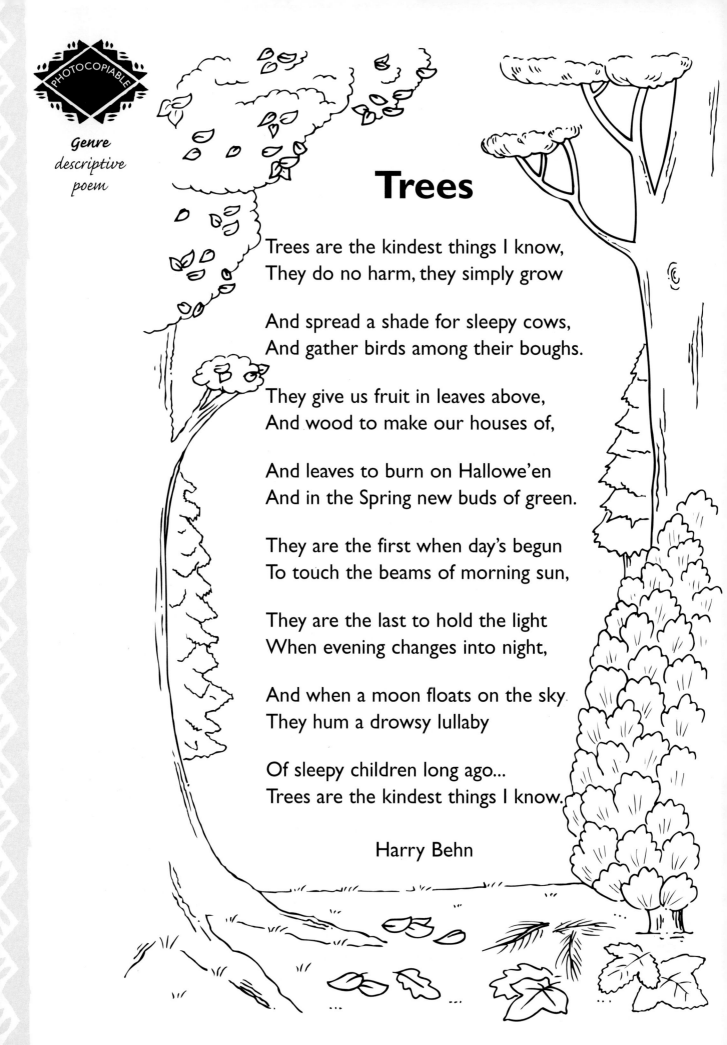

Trees

Ideally, this text should be read with the children on a pleasant spring or summer's day while sitting beneath the shade of a tree. Collect pictures of a variety of mature trees, and a collection of items made of wood.

This poem points out the usefulness of trees and encourages children to take notice of familiar things they see every day.

Science learning objectives

◆ To explore, using the senses of sight, smell and touch, and make and record observations (Sc1 2f).

◆ To recognize and name the leaf, flower, stem and root of flowering plants (Sc2 3b).

◆ To group living things according to observable similarities and differences (Sc2 4b).

◆ To find out about the different kinds of plants and animals in the local environment (Sc2 5a).

◆ To recognize and name common types of material and know that some of them are found naturally (Sc3 1c).

◆ To find out about the uses of various materials and relate these to their simple properties (Sc3 1d).

Discussing the text

◆ Help the children to appreciate that this is a gentle, quiet poem, and that trees are usually still and quiet. Relate this a nearby tree that the children see every day: it is always there, making no fuss, being ignored and taken for granted by us. Yet trees are busy getting on with their lives.

◆ Ask the children to identify useful things that trees do which the poet mentions. Can they think of any others?

◆ Talk about the Sun and the tree. Do the children know why the poet, Harry Behn, should think that a tree is the first thing to catch the morning Sun and the last to hold on to the Sun's light in the evening? Perhaps it is because trees are usually so tall and seem to reach upwards. Are trees the tallest things the children can see? If not, what is taller?

◆ Is it a good description to say that the moon floats on the sky? Have any of the children seen this for themselves? When the moon is full, remind them to look outside and see what they think.

◆ Explain that a 'lullaby' is a song that people sing to babies to send them to sleep. Can the children suggest how a tree might 'hum' a lullaby?

Vocabulary

Trunk, stem, branch, root, leaf, leaves, flower, fruit, wood, natural, tall, taller, tallest.

Science activities

◆ Provide a large drawing of a tree and separate labels reading *trunk, roots, leaves, branches, flower* and *fruit*. Encourage the children to identify the parts and attach the labels correctly. Explain that the trunk of a tree is like the *stem* of a smaller plant; and that many trees have very small green flowers that are difficult to see, while others (such as apple trees) have masses of white blossom.

◆ If appropriate take the class on a walk around the school grounds, the neighbourhood or (ideally) a small wood, and look at the different types of tree. Ask the children whether they can sort the trees into groups in any way; they may suggest the type of leaves, texture of bark, overall shape or (depending on the time of year) the flowers or fruits.

◆ As a class, 'adopt' a nearby tree. Visit it regularly and make careful observations. Start a tree diary, including drawings and photographs to represent a year in the life of the tree. This will become a useful record, providing scientific evidence that will be of value to others. Make a list of the useful things the tree does: it might shade the playground, provide places for birds to rest, provide food for caterpillars, or provide hiding-places in its bark for very small creatures.

◆ Ask the children to draw a tree in the middle of a page and surround it with words and drawings to show how useful it is (see illustration below).

◆ Explain that wood is a natural material because it comes from a tree and is not made by humans. Ask the children to point out things around them that are made of wood. How do they know the material is wood? Talk about how we use our senses to recognize wood. Ask a group of children to organize a game where they identify wooden objects from a selection of items, using touch only.

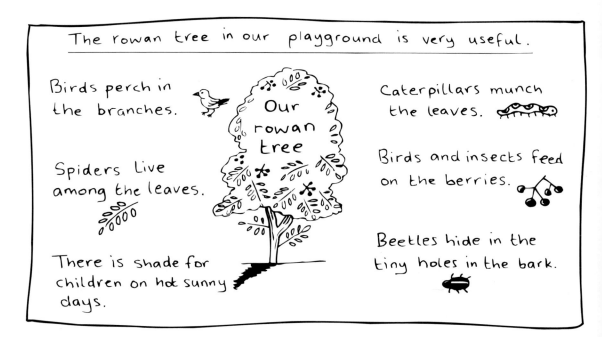

The rowan tree in our playground is very useful.

Birds perch in the branches.

Spiders live among the leaves.

There is shade for children on hot sunny days.

Our rowan tree

Caterpillars munch the leaves.

Birds and insects feed on the berries.

Beetles hide in the tiny holes in the bark.

Further literacy ideas

◆ Identify the rhyming words in the poem. You could read it out again, asking the children to join in with the last word of each line. Ask the children how they can tell which words rhyme. Choose some rhyming pairs of words and encourage the children to think of further rhymes – for example: *know, grow, mow, go, so, blow* and *lullaby, sky, dry, high, my, why*.

◆ Encourage the children to write about their own feelings about trees, perhaps describing a tree they know well. Some children might like to add a pair of rhyming lines of their own to Harry Behn's poem.

◆ Organize a performance of the poem, with the children taking part individually or in groups. Encourage them to create the gentle, soothing feelings of the poem – by the last line, everyone should be feeling sleepy!

◆ Ask the children to make labels for a collection of wooden items. Point out how this information might be useful to others.

◆ Encourage the children to use the words *tall, taller* and *tallest* in describing trees or buildings that they can see locally.

◆ Focus on the words *leaf* and *leaves*; encourage the children to remember how to spell these words.

Ten Tall Oaktrees

Genre
counting
poem

Ten tall oaktrees
Standing in a line,
'Warships,' cried King Henry,
Then there were nine.

Nine tall oaktrees
Growing strong and straight,
'Charcoal,' breathed the furnace,
Then there were eight.

Eight tall oaktrees
Reaching towards heaven,
'Sizzle,' spoke the lightning,
Then there were seven.

Seven tall oaktrees,
Branches, leaves and sticks,
'Firewood,' smiled the merchant,
Then there were six.

Six tall oaktrees
Glad to be alive
'Barrels,' boomed the brewery,
Then there were five.

Five tall oaktrees,
Suddenly a roar,
'Gangway,' screamed the west wind,
Then there were four.

Four tall oaktrees
Sighing like the sea,
'Floorboards,' beamed the builder,
Then there were three.

Three tall oaktrees
Groaning as trees do,
'Unsafe,' claimed the council,
Then there were two.

Two tall oaktrees
Spreading in the sun,
'Progress,' snarled the by-pass,
Then there was one.

One tall oaktree
Wishing it could run,
'Nuisance,' grumped the farmer,
Then there were none.

No tall oaktrees,
Search the fields in vain,
Only empty skylines
And the cold grey rain.

Richard Edwards

Ten Tall Oaktrees

This poem describes the fate of many trees. It can be used to introduce the theme of conserving and using natural resources and caring for the environment.

Display pictures of different mature trees. Cut out the outlines of ten large trees (to use when performing the poem). Make a collection of tree seeds, including acorns, nuts, sycamore keys, haws, apple pips and fruit stones. Display the collection of wooden items from the previous activity (see page 76).

Science learning objectives

◆ To recognise the importance of collecting evidence (Sc1 1).
◆ To recognize that plants need light and water to grow (Sc2 3a).
◆ To know that seeds grow into flowering plants (Sc2 3c).
◆ To care for the environment (Sc2 5c).
◆ To find out about the uses of a variety of materials, and how these uses are related to their simple properties (Sc3 1d).
◆ To encourage observation and exploration and the recording of observation and measurements (Sc1 2a, b, f).

Discussing the text

◆ Make sure the children understand the theme of the poem: that over a period of time, ten tall trees eventually disappear. Read the verses separately and discuss what happened to each tree. The children might like to imagine themselves as one of the trees. For which purpose would they prefer to be cut down?

◆ Pick out the words that have been used to rhyme with the numbers. Underline these in the text, and ask the children to chant them – thus counting backwards from ten to 'none'.

◆ Help the children to recognize the structure of the poem. Go through the poem, reading only the third line of each verse, perhaps with the children joining in to say the spoken words: 'Warships', 'Charcoal' and so on.

◆ How does the poet, Richard Edwards, feel about trees? Do the children think he likes them? Is he sad when they are all cut down?

Vocabulary

Tall, taller, tallest, grow, wood, seeds, light, water, uses, useful.

Science activities

◆ Discuss the reasons for the disappearance of the trees in the poem.
Group the reasons, perhaps into: needing wood for its uses; the weather; because they were in the way.

◆ Refer to the collection of wooden items and talk about why wood is such a useful material. Make a list of its properties. Focus on its uses over the years: building boats (it is strong, will float, and can be cut to the right size); building houses (it is strong and light in weight, and can be cut and shaped); as a fuel (it burns easily, but not too fast). The children can write a page or poster describing the uses of wood.

◆ Find a nearby vantage point and spot the trees. Are there a few, many or a lot? How would the children feel if the trees were removed? Would it matter? Are trees more useful when they are alive or when they are cut down for use? Encourage the children to think about the loss to the wildlife of the neighbourhood, particularly the creatures deprived of a home or food.

◆ During discussion, the children might suggest that more trees should be planted to replace ones that are cut down. Encourage them to think of planting trees as a valuable activity. Point out that in a controlled forest, old trees are cut down to allow new ones to grow. If appropriate, organize a tree planting session in the school grounds (perhaps to commemorate an event). In autumn, the children can collect tree seeds and plant them in pots, care for the seedlings and record their progress. Eventually, the young trees can be planted in gardens or hedgerows. The children can record what they have done and what they observe, including photographs (see illustration below).

Planting our tree

We decided on a good place to plant the oak tree that we had grown from a seed.

We dug a hole.

Carefully we took the tree and its soil out of the pot and planted it in the hole.

Then we filled in the hole and watered our tree.

We took a photograph of our tree.

We are going to look after our special oak tree and see how well it grows.

 spring    summer    autumn   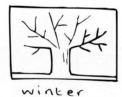 winter

Further literacy ideas

◆ Make a chart of four columns to record rhyming words: the first column for the numbers from ten to none, the second for the rhyming words in the poem (except for 'ten'), and the last two for children to contribute their own ideas. The chart can be a class effort or the children can work on their own charts with some words already recorded to help them get started.

◆ Create a wall display to tell the story of the ten trees. Children can contribute by writing the numbers and other labels to explain what is happening.

◆ Find the word in each verse that describes how the spoken words were delivered: *cried, breathed, spoke, smiled* and so on. The children could imitate these with sounds and facial expressions as the poem is read out.

◆ Practise the whole poem for a performance. Each group or individuals can recite the same part of each verse, such as the first line, the last line or the spoken words. Use the large cut-out trees to demonstrate the sequence of the trees' disappearance.

◆ Ask the children what they notice about the first and last words of each verse (except the last verse). To highlight the pattern made by these words, the children could draw coloured circles around them.

Genre
poem

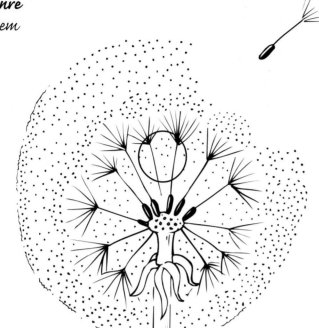

Dandelion

Nobody winds the dandelion,
nobody oils his clock,
nobody counts his timely beat
tick... tick... tock.

Nobody sets the right alarm,
nobody holds his key,
nobody tells him what to do –
where to be.

Nobody fixes every seed
so, in a perfect ball,
each in his individual place –
nobody bids them fall...

Only a wind, a bit of a breeze,
only a wandering whim
blows him this or the other way –
roots and anchors him.

Jean Kenward

Dandelion

Read this poem when there are plenty of dandelion seedheads about and the children have the opportunity to look closely at these plants, asking questions themselves. Provide a selection of clocks for the children to see, including one that needs a key to wind it up.

This poem uses the traditional image of the 'dandelion clock' to explore the nature of a plant.

Science learning objectives

◆ To recognise the importance of collecting evidence by making observations when trying to answer a question (Sc1 1).

◆ To relate life processes to plants found in the local environment (Sc2 1c).

◆ To recognize that plants need light and water to grow (Sc2 3a).

◆ To recognize and name the leaf, flower, stem and root of flowering plants (Sc2 3b).

◆ To know that seeds grow into flowering plants (Sc2 3c).

Discussing the text

◆ Find out whether the children know that the seedhead of a dandelion is known as a 'dandelion clock'; if necessary, explain that this refers to a traditional game of 'telling the time' by blowing dandelion seeds. At an appropriate time, perhaps before reading the text, take the children to search for dandelion clocks and demonstrate this game.

◆ Identify the actions associated with mechanical clocks that are mentioned by Jean Kenward: winding, oiling, the tick-tock sound, setting the alarm, using a key to wind the mechanism. Point out that she is asking how the dandelion clock can 'work' without anyone doing these things.

◆ Show the children a dandelion clock or a large picture of one, and read the third verse again so that the children can appreciate the 'perfect ball' with every seed fixed carefully in place.

◆ Ask the children what does make the dandelion clock work (besides themselves when they blow). Help them to understand the last verse, where the poet is explaining how the seeds are spread.

◆ Point out the play on words: *winds* in the first verse (referring to a clock) and *wind* in the last verse (referring to the breeze). Emphasize the difference in sound between these two words.

Vocabulary

Grow, water, root, leaves, stem, flower, bud, seed.

Science activities

◆ As dandelion plants are very common, it should be possible to find some on a walk around the school grounds or the immediate neighbourhood. Before the search, ask the children how they will recognize the plant (its bright yellow flowers, 'clocks' and jagged, dark green leaves).

◆ Dig up some whole plants and wash the roots, so that the children can examine each part of the plant. A whole plant can be kept in a jar of water for observation, and the children can draw and label a root, leaf, stem and flower. Remind the children that a dandelion is a plant which is a living thing: it will die if it is deprived of water and light.

◆ Try to find dandelion flowers in different stages of development to show the children the sequence from bud to seedhead. Point out that unless there are flowers, there will be no seeds. Draw simple pictures of the four stages of flower development for the children to put in order: green bud, open flower, dying flower, seedhead.

◆ Provide hand lenses so that the children can examine individual seeds. The difficulty they will have in handling these will demonstrate how light and fragile they are. Draw a large picture of a seed for the children to copy and label; they can attach a real seed to the same sheet of paper with clear tape to show the actual size. Consider how many seeds each plant produces. Ask the children why the dandelion is so common and why it is regarded as a nuisance by gardeners.

◆ Help the children to work out the stages in the life of a dandelion plant. Make a large cyclical diagram to illustrate this (see illustration).

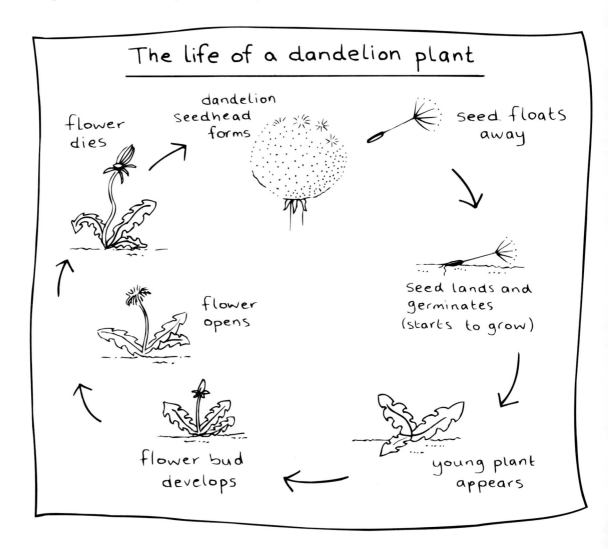

Further literacy ideas

◆ Underline the word 'nobody' each time it occurs in the poem; as you read the poem, encourage the children to repeat this word with you.

◆ Ask the children to suggest why the plant is called 'dandelion'. Could it be that the bright yellow flowers remind people of lions' manes? Do the leaves of the plant look like lions' teeth?

◆ Can the children identify the rhymes in the poem? Do they remember any other poem with rhymes arranged in this way?

◆ Suggest writing a similar poem (which does not need to rhyme) to tell the reader how to help spread the dandelion seeds by blowing the clock.

How to grow a giant pumpkin

Genre
instructions

Sow a seed in spring, keep an eye on your plant through the summer, and you could have a giant pumpkin to harvest in the autumn.

You will need:
- a seed from a giant pumpkin
- a plant pot
- some compost
- a label and sticky tape.

The seed will need:
- water
- warmth
- special care.

What to do:

1. Write your name and the date on a label and fasten it to the pot.

2. Put compost in the pot until it is nearly full.

3. Carefully make a hole in the compost with your finger.

4. Put the seed in the hole.

5. Pinch the soil to cover the seed.

6. Give the seed water whenever the compost is dry.

7. Keep the pot in a warm place.

8. When the leaves appear, make sure the young plant has plenty of light.

When the plant has several leaves, it can be planted in the garden.

ALWAYS wash your hands after handling compost and working with plants.

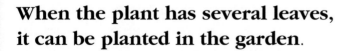

How to grow a giant pumpkin

These instructions encourage children to sow a seed and nurture a plant.

Display pictures of pumpkins, and obtain seeds from packets (or saved from last year's fruit). Use peat-free compost. When the seeds are planted, cover the pots with cling film to prevent them from drying out while germination occurs. Seeds planted at the beginning of the summer term should be ready for planting out by half term.

Science learning objectives

◆ To recognise the importance of making observations and measurements when trying to answer a question (Sc1 1).

◆ To carry out a complete investigation (Sc1 2a–j).

◆ To know that plants need light and water to grow (Sc2 3a).

◆ To recognize and name the leaf, flower, stem and root of a flowering plant (Sc2 3b).

◆ To know that seeds grow into flowering plants (Sc2 3c).

Discussing the text

◆ Find out whether the children know what a pumpkin is. Where might they have seen one? Show them pictures, or draw and cut out the outline of a pumpkin, so that they appreciate the size of the fruit that could grow from a single seed.

◆ Relate the sequence of events to the seasons of the year.

◆ Encourage the children to comment on the layout of the text. Ask how it is different from a story. How useful is it to have the things you need listed at the beginning? Is it a good idea to have numbered points to work from?

◆ Ask the children to mime the actions while you read the instructions, as a kind of rehearsal for the real activity.

Vocabulary

Seed, light, water, grow, compost, leaves, seedling, dark.

Science activities

◆ Give the children a seed each to examine. Pumpkin seeds are relatively large and quite easy to handle. Ask them to observe the tough skin that protects the beginnings of the root and shoot. Explain that the seed will remain in this state until water and warmth cause it to spring into action. Allow a seed to germinate on moist tissue so that the children can observe the process of germination.

◆ Make a collection of seeds, such as dried peas and beans, small flower seeds from seed packets, acorns, fruit pips, honesty and teasel seeds. Warn the children that although some seeds are edible, others are very poisonous and none must be eaten without an adult's consent. The children can use hand lenses to examine and compare the seeds, then sort them into order of size and record which seeds are bigger than a pumpkin seed and which are smaller.

◆ Allow each child to follow the instructions and grow their own pumpkin plant. Sow a few extra seeds in case of germination failure. Encourage daily observation. The children can make a diary of their observations. Insist on accurate recording, use of scientific vocabulary, and measurement if appropriate. Take photographs as the plants develop.

◆ Encourage the children to care for the individual plants. Remind them that the seed needed water and warmth so that it could begin to grow, and the young plants also need light. Ask the children for ideas about how they might test whether seedlings need light to grow well. Suggest using cress seedlings (ones that the children have already grown or ready-grown ones from a greengrocer). Put half the seedlings in a cupboard or a dark part of the room and the rest in the brightest spot. Talk about the need for both sets of seedlings to be treated in exactly the same way, apart from their positions, so that the results of the test will be of value. Prepare a sheet on which the children can record the process and results of their investigation.

Further literacy ideas

◆ To remind the children of the sequence of the seasons, encourage them to draw a set of three pictures with captions to show the times of sowing, growing and harvesting the pumpkin.

◆ Help the children to recognize and underline the command word in each instruction in the text.

◆ Ask the children to write a set of instructions for something they can do well, such as feeding a pet or using a mechanical toy.

◆ The children can write an account of their seed sowing and describe the progress of their plant.

Caring for your pumpkin plant

Genre
instructions

When your pumpkin plant has several leaves, it can be planted out in the garden.

You will need:
- the pumpkin plant
- a small trowel
- some manure or fertilizer
- old gloves
- a watering can.

The plant will need:
- plenty of room to grow
- a good supply of water
- sunny days
- protection from slugs and other animals.

How to care for your pumpkin plant:

1. Decide on a sunny spot, sheltered from the wind, in the garden.

2. Put on some old gloves, and use a small trowel to dig a fairly big hole.

3. Put the manure or fertilizer in the hole and cover it with some soil.

4. Carefully remove the pumpkin plant from its pot and plant it firmly, covering the roots with soil.

5. Water the plant well. Young pumpkin plants need plenty of water, and will probably need watering every day that it does not rain.

6. Keep an eye on your plant during its early life. It will soon produce yellow flowers which will turn into pumpkins.

7. Watch the pumpkins grow bigger during the summer, and harvest them in the autumn.

A tip: Look out for slugs which like to nibble pumpkins. Slide a piece of plastic under the fruits as they grow to keep them off the soil and away from slugs.

Wear gloves when handling soil and **ALWAYS** wash your hands after gardening.

Good luck!

Caring for your pumpkin plant

These instructions follow on from the previous text. They show children how to continue the care of their pumpkin plant.

Organize alternative arrangements for children without a suitable garden. This could mean allocating a patch of ground around the school for pumpkin growing, or finding guardians (owners of some spare ground) for the plants. Encourage the children to enlist the help of parents and grandparents, who might have extra advice on growing a giant pumpkin.

The first two leaves that emerge from the seed are not true leaves but the seed leaves; these are different in shape from the true leaves.

Science learning objectives

◆ To make and record observations (Sc1 2f).
◆ To relate life processes to plants found in the local environment (Sc2 1c).
◆ To know that humans and other animals need food and water to stay alive (Sc2 2b).
◆ To know that plants need light and water to grow (Sc2 3a).
◆ To recognize and name the leaf, flower, stem and root of flowering plants (Sc2 3b).
◆ To find out about the different kinds of plants and animals in the local environment (Sc2 5a).

Discussing the text

◆ If the children have successfully reared a young pumpkin plant, they will be keen to know how to care for it during the next stage of its life. Do they think the instructions will be useful when they try to look after the plant at home? Would they know what to do without the instructions? Would they remember everything if the instructions were only spoken? Ask who else might find the instructions useful (perhaps the person who will help them in the garden).

◆ Find out what the children think *manure or fertilizer* is. Why is it needed? Take this opportunity of reminding them to wear gloves when handling soil, manure or fertilizer, and always to wash their hands afterwards even if they think their hands look clean – germs are invisible!

◆ Do the children recognize the layout of the instructions? Does the text look similar to any text they have seen before? Will they be able to follow the instructions when they get home?

◆ Explain that a sunny spot that is sheltered from the wind is likely to be against a south-facing wall or fence. The hole should be up to 45cm deep and 60cm wide.

◆ Find out whether the children understand what a 'tip' is. What is the purpose of this part of the instructions? (To provide an extra idea that might be useful.)

◆ Why do the children think they will need good luck? Point out that when we are looking after plants, things do not always go to plan: the weather might affect the plants badly, animals or careless people might walk on the young plant, minibeasts might eat the leaves or the fruit, and so on. Prepare the children for possible disappointment so that they do not become too upset if their plant does not thrive.

◆ Read out the instructions again, and encourage the children to mime each point with you as a rehearsal for the actual planting.

Vocabulary

Grow, leaves, stem, roots, flowers, fruit, water, sunlight, changes, protect, manure, fertilizer, harvest.

Science activities

◆ Encourage the children to examine and draw the plant they have grown, labelling the leaves and stem and indicating where the roots are. Remove one plant from its pot to show how the roots have grown.

◆ Discuss the future needs of the plant when it is in the garden. Explain that a pumpkin plant needs more water than a lot of plants, and ask how this plant will get the water it needs. Rain provides water but what can the children do on dry days?

◆ Point out that many plants we like to have in our gardens would not normally grow in this country and need caring for if they are going to produce flowers or fruits. The pumpkin is an example.

◆ Ask the children to predict the changes that will take place when the plant is in the garden. The plant will get bigger, more leaves will grow, flowers will develop, the flowers will die and the fruits (pumpkins) will begin to grow. Explain that they will be small at first, the size of a marble, but could grow to be huge – especially if given extra fertilizer which contains minerals that will keep them strong. Prepare the children for failure, as weather conditions and animals will often damage and kill the plants.

◆ Talk about how we grow pumpkins for food: to make pies and to use as a vegetable. Ask the children to think of other plants that we grow for food. Discuss why it is important for humans to grow plants for food. The children can make a poster or chart to show plants that are useful for providing food, such as apple trees, bean and tomato plants, carrots and potatoes.

◆ Refer to other animals beside humans that like to eat the plants we grow. Slugs, caterpillars, mice and some birds annoy us by eating 'our' food plants. Talk about a garden as an environment where different animals and plants live. The children could predict what animals and plants their pumpkin plant will share its environment with, then observe and record.

Further literacy ideas

◆ Encourage the children to look closely at each instruction and see whether they can spot and underline the main word that tells them what to do (for example: *decide, use, put, remove...*).

◆ Encourage the children to write a set of instructions to help other children with some school-related activity.

◆ Collect the words in the text beginning with the letter **p**. Add others then use them to create a tongue-twister.

Riddles: Plants

Genre
riddles

I cannot move around.
But if you give me the chance, I can grow quite tall.
I give homes to birds and beetles.
What am I?

You can find me growing everywhere.
I have a bright yellow head,
And I can help you tell the time.
What am I?

I am a special kind of plant.
I like to grow in dry places.
So do not give me too much water,
And beware my spiky body.
What am I?

Look in hedgerows in autumn
For black shiny fruits,
Making your fingers purple as you pick.
At night, scurrying mouse and snuffling fox
Enjoy my snacks as much as you do.
What am I?

These small parcels are very valuable.
Soon the wrapping will burst
And a plant will appear.
It could have a bright flower, a tasty vegetable, a juicy fruit.
Perhaps it will become a magnificent tree.
What are these valuable parcels?

Riddles: Plants

These riddles introduce children to word puzzles, and encourage them to look for clues to the answers.

Present the riddles one at a time, letting the children focus their attention on each.

Science learning objectives

◆ To be aware of the parts, growth and reproduction of green plants, their diversity and their role in the local environment (Sc2 1c; 3a, b, c; 4b; 5a, b).

◆ To use simple scientific language to communicate ideas and to name and describe living things (Breadth of study 2a).

Responding to the text

◆ Choose a riddle to read to the children - perhaps as an introduction to a science topic, in relation to current science work or as revision. At this stage, keep out of sight any pictures or plants to be used with later discussion.

◆ For each riddle, reveal the lines one at a time so that the children have plenty of time to think about each clue.

◆ Focus on the question mark at the end of each riddle and explain that an answer is required. Encourage the children to provide the answer in the form of a sentence rather than a single word.

◆ Point out that **all** the clues in each riddle should be considered to arrive at an answer.

Riddle 1

◆ Read the first line and compare plants (which cannot usually move from place to place) with animals (which can travel around).

◆ Read the first two lines and ask the children to name plants they know that can grow quite tall. They might look out of the window for inspiration. Write down some of their ideas.

◆ Read the next line and highlight any of the first suggestions that are still appropriate.

◆ Decide on a suitable answer, such as 'You are a tree'. Some children might like to name a specific tree, perhaps one that they see every day.

Riddle 2

◆ After reading the first line, see whether the children can name any common plants. They might suggest grass, trees and weeds.

◆ Guide the children towards thinking of plants with a yellow flowerhead, giving extra clues if necessary.

◆ The final clue will help the children to decide on the answer, especially if they have heard the poem 'Dandelion' by Jean Kenward (see page 80) and have enjoyed blowing dandelion seeds.

Riddle 3

◆ Read the first two lines and see whether the children have any ideas about the kind of plant this riddle is describing. It might be useful to discuss and eliminate plants that require plenty of water, such as seaweeds, pond plants or any classroom plants that wilt easily.

◆ Read the rest of the riddle. If the children do not suggest a cactus plant, draw a simple illustration as an extra clue.

Riddle 4

◆ Remind the children what is meant by a hedgerow. Do they have any experience of looking for fruits in the autumn?

◆ Explain that this riddle describes a wild fruit that is safe to eat, but that other berries the children may see must not be tasted as many are poisonous to humans.

◆ When the children have decided that the riddle is describing blackberries, point out that the clues actually refer to the plant bearing the blackberries: a blackberry bush, also known as a bramble (or perhaps by a familiar local name).

Riddle 5

◆ After reading the first three lines of the riddle, ask the children whether they have any ideas about what is being described.

◆ Read the rest of the riddle; if necessary, remind the children of any seed-sowing they have done.

◆ Ask the children why the seeds are described as 'valuable'.

Vocabulary

Plants, flower, fruit, seed, leaf, leaves, stem, root, question, answer, clue.

Science activities

Riddle 1

◆ On a walk around the school grounds or immediate neighbourhood, identify the tallest tree. Decide whether the trees are taller than nearby buildings. Emphasize that trees are plants, and find a small plant (not a shrub) to compare with a tree.

◆ Focus on a nearby tree and discover which animals use it, whether for perching, hiding or feeding.

Riddle 2

◆ Search for dandelion plants. Identify the leaves, stem, flower and seeds (if the season is appropriate). Dig up a plant to show the roots. Ask the children to draw the plant and label its parts.

◆ Talk about how the seeds travel, blown by the wind. Can the children explain why dandelion plants are found almost everywhere?

Riddle 3

◆ Provide a collection of cacti and succulent plants, warning the children not to touch those with spikes or sharp hairs. Compare cacti with more familiar plants, pointing out the great diversity among plants.

◆ Talk about how convenient cacti are as house plants: they can be left for days, perhaps while you go on holiday, without needing to be watered.

Riddle 4

◆ Arrange a visit to a hedgerow so that the children can observe the different plants and small creatures that live there. If fruits are developing, take the opportunity to warn the children against tasting any of them. Identify blackberries as a safe fruit, but remind the children that they should only sample them if given permission by an adult. At other times of the year, look for the spiky stems of the bramble and the white flowers from which the fruit will develop.

Riddle 5

◆ Provide a collection of seeds for the children to examine. Encourage the children to think of them as parcels, with the contents waiting to emerge as a young plant.

◆ Plant a variety of seeds so that the children can observe the growth of the seedlings. Peas, beans and cress grow well in pots. Seeds of trees and garden plants can be started in pots and then planted out in gardens.

◆ During the summer and autumn, look for interesting seeds developing on plants such as sycamore trees, thistles, rosebay willowherb, honesty and teasels. Encourage the children to think about how these seeds will be scattered.

Further literacy ideas

Riddle 1

◆ Ask the children to supply new clues for a riddle about a tree which can be read other classes.

◆ Use trees to make comparisons using the words *tall, taller* and *tallest*.

Riddle 2

◆ Ask the children to look in the school grounds for plants and use these to compose their own riddles for others to solve. Suggest using the first line of the original riddle as a starter, perhaps changing the word 'everywhere' to a more specific location.

Riddle 3

◆ Provide a selection of potted plants for the children to describe using riddles. Other children can be asked to match each plant with its riddle.

◆ Talk about opposites, especially *wet* and *dry*, *spiky* and *smooth* and perhaps *dangerous* and *safe*.

◆ Ask the children to identify a word in the riddle beginning with 'pl'. Make a collection of other 'pl' words.

Riddle 4

◆ Identify aspects of autumn; make a collage of the characteristics of this season, including local events or traditions.

◆ Identify words in the riddle beginning with 'sn', 'bl', 'sh' and 'sc'. Collect other words that begin in the same way.

Riddle 5

◆ Make a list, with illustrations, of flowers, vegetables and fruits that the children know.

◆ Ask the children to change the words (adjectives) used to describe a flower, vegetable, fruit and tree for ones of their own.

◆ Talk about things that the children consider to be valuable. Emphasize that the word does not always refer to money.

Materials

Materials are all around us. Throughout history, people have learned about the properties of these materials – both natural and manufactured – and discovered innumerable ways of using them.

The texts in this chapter help children to explore the range of familiar materials available to us, and demonstrate some of the uses we make of them. They introduce the children to the oldest materials on the Earth, as well as to materials specially made for our purposes. The children are encouraged to use their senses to examine familiar objects in everyday situations, identifying the materials that have been used to make them, recognizing their properties, and investigating similarities and differences. Some texts provide opportunities for the children to sort common objects according to the materials from which they are made, or the properties of those materials.

Some of the texts remind the children how materials can change or be changed in everyday situations – for example, by squashing, heating or cooling. The texts help to introduce the children to ways in which these processes affect our lives. Opportunities arise through the texts in this chapter for the children to observe and explore changing materials, experiencing for themselves the changes that take place as a result of heating and cooling.

They are encouraged to ask questions, to make simple predictions, to follow instructions and to discuss and record their findings.

Useful links with other areas of science are made, particularly relating to how we use our senses to become aware of the immediate environment: observing movements and exploring sounds.

The children are reminded of the hazards encountered when working with very hot and cold materials, and ways of reducing risks to themselves and others are highlighted.

PHOTOCOPIABLE

Genre
*poem with
rhyme and
rhythm*

Stones

I like stones.
I like to touch
their shape and colour:
such, and such.
Lift one up
and you may find
tiny creatures
there confined
hidden safely
out of sight
in a small
and private night.

Stones are quiet,
stones are cold.
Some of them
are old – so old
that upon
their surface clings
a pattern of
the strangest things:
leaves, and fish,
and shells and seas
and birds from different
skies than these
when the Earth
had just begun.

Stones know more
than anyone.

Jean Kenward

Stones

Collect and display a variety of pebbles and stones, including some that show fossils.

Science learning objectives

◆ Know the differences between things that are living and things that have never been alive (Sc2 1a).

◆ To identify similarities and differences between local environments and ways in which these affect animals and plants that are found there (Sc2 5b).

◆ To use their senses to explore and recognize the similarities and differences between materials (Sc3 1a).

◆ To sort objects into groups on the basis of simple material properties (Sc3 1b).

◆ To recognize and name common types of material and know that some of them are found naturally (Sc3 1c).

◆ To find out about the uses of materials and how these are related to their simple properties (Sc3 1d).

Discussing the text

◆ Ask the children how they know this text is a poem. They should recognize the rhyme and rhythm.

◆ Give the children a pebble or stone each, so that they can feel its texture and consider its history while the poem is re-read.

◆ Emphasize the age of the stones the children have in their hands: point out that they are holding some of the oldest things on the Earth.

◆ Explain that the patterns on the rocks that Jean Kenward describes are fossils, which give us clues to the kinds of animals and plants that lived on the Earth millions of years ago.

◆ The poet tells us that stones are quiet. Encourage the children to imagine what stories the stones could tell about the distant past.

Vocabulary

Living, not living, animals, fossils, rock, natural, materials, dark, damp.

Science activities

◆ Ask the children to imagine putting a stone next to a small animal that might be mistaken for a pebble when it is still, such as a mouse, spider or woodlouse. Ask them to draw a pebble and an animal, and to write down how they could tell the difference. They should mention that the animal will eventually move away, while the stone will remain in place (probably forever); the animal will need to find food and shelter and will grow and change, while the stone does none of these things.

◆ Take the children out to find what is living under stones in the school grounds. If appropriate, arrange some large stones in suitable places a week before this activity. Emphasize that the children should remove the stones carefully, so as not to disturb the animals and their home too much, and should replace them just as they were found. Make a chart to show the range of animals found, or

This poem encourages children to consider stones, which as familiar objects are often ignored or taken for granted.

their frequency. Accurate names are not essential: 'large black beetle' and 'small white grub' are acceptable descriptions.

◆ Talk about the chart and ask the children why these particular animals chose to live or shelter there. They must all prefer the same conditions of dark and damp. Perhaps they feel safe from their enemies there, or perhaps they are looking for food in these dark spaces.

◆ Ask the children to help you build up a collection of small pieces of rock (which they might also call stones or pebbles). Find different ways of sorting these, perhaps according to: shape; pattern; whether they have fossils, crystals or holes; whether they are rough or smooth. Help the children to distinguish between natural materials and pieces of man-made products such as brick and concrete.

◆ Encourage the children to examine different rocks and describe their properties. Remind them of words such as *hard, strong, rough, smooth* and *firm*. Talk about how difficult it is to change a rock in any way. It cannot be bent or squeezed. Discuss what sort of tools you would need to alter the rocks.

◆ Ask the children to think of uses for rocks. They might suggest building walls or houses, decorating gardens, holding things down and so on. They may also think of precious stones used in jewellery. Collect small items made from rocks (such as ornaments, slates and items of jewellery) for the children to examine.

Further literacy ideas

◆ Look at the words *stones, rocks* and *pebbles*. Explain that these are all words that mean pieces of the Earth, but that pebbles are usually smooth because they have been worn smooth by the sea's waves (like a bar of soap of soap used in the shower). Find words to rhyme (or nearly rhyme) with these words, such as *bones, socks* and *wobbles*; encourage the children to invent two lines of nonsense verse.

◆ The children can adopt a favourite stone, describe it and imagine its history. Perhaps it was washed up on the sand where early ships landed, provided a home for a community of slugs, or was used to build an ancient tower.

◆ Write out labels with words and phrases that the children have used to describe the stones in the class collection. Pairs of children can take turns to match the labels with the stones in a display.

◆ Read out the poem once more, and encourage the children to join in the last two lines with you as a finale.

Sorting my toys

'You must sort out your toys today,' said Mum.

I went to my room.

I opened my toy box.

I sorted my toys.

In one pile I put my jigsaws, my puzzle books and my teddy. These are my quiet toys. In another pile I put my drum, my whistle, my hammer and my singing elephant. These are my noisy toys. I played with my noisy toys.

'Stop that din!' shouted Mum. 'Sort out your toys!'

I sorted my toys again.

In one pile I put my wheelbarrow, my tractor and some of my cars. I push these toys when I play with them. In another pile I put my duck on wheels, my fluffy dog on a lead and my horse and cart. I pull these toys when I play with them. I played with my push and pull toys.

'Have you sorted your toys yet?' called Mum.

I sorted my toys again.

In one pile I put my toys made of wood – my train, my garage, my doll and my cricket bat. In another pile I put my toys made of plastic – my cars, my bucket and spade and my plastic people.

Mum came into my room.

'What a mess!' she cried. 'Why haven't you sorted your toys?'

What did she mean?

Sorting my toys

This text reminds children that there are different ways of grouping things.

Prepare collections of assorted items which the children can sort according to their own criteria.

Science learning objectives

◆ To use their senses to explore and recognize the similarities and differences between materials (Sc3 1a).

◆ To sort objects into groups on the basis of simple material properties (Sc3 1b).

◆ To recognize and name common types of material (Sc3 1c).

◆ To find out about the uses of a variety of materials and link these to their simple properties (Sc3 1d).

◆ To know that both pushes and pulls are examples of forces (Sc4 2b).

◆ To know that there are many kinds of sound and sources of sound (Sc4 3c).

Discussing the text

◆ What do the children think 'Mum' in the story meant when she said the toys needed sorting out? (Perhaps she expected the child to put things in boxes, collect broken parts or throw away anything unwanted.) Did the child do what Mum wanted? Why was the child puzzled?

◆ Ask the children whether they too have trouble keeping their toys in order. How do toys come to be jumbled up? Do they have they any good ideas for keeping things tidy which they can share?

◆ Do the children think the child is a boy or a girl? What evidence do they have? Is it possible to be sure?

◆ What noisy toys do the children have? Are there times when they only play with quiet toys? (Perhaps if someone is ill, or when people in the room are talking.)

◆ Ask the children to suggest ideas for sorting their toys – they might think of sorting by colour, by size, or by whether they are favourite toys.

Vocabulary

Materials, plastic, wood, metal, paper, fabric, rock, glass, noise, noisy, quiet, sounds, push, pull.

Science activities

◆ Ask the children what toys they would put in the groups described in the text. What quiet and noisy toys do they have? What push and pull toys? Can they think of other wood and plastic toys?

◆ Provide pairs or small groups with a box of miscellaneous items and ask them to sort these things in any way they like. Include objects such as a pencil, notebook, piece of twig, leaf, wooden block, stone, plastic toy, glove and piece of string. Accept all suggested criteria. Ask the children to label and record their groupings and to explain their reasons to each other.

◆ Create displays around the room of things made of different materials, such as plastic, wood, paper, fabric, rock and glass. Encourage the children to contribute small items to the displays and to draw and add pictures of large things such as a car, a door, a chair or a window.

◆ Ask the children to group unseen items, using blindfolds or feely bags. Can they identify wood, metal and paper by touch and give their reasons?

◆ Display items that make a sound, such as a range of musical instruments and things that rattle, bleep or can be tapped. Ask the children to list these according to the type of sound they make.

◆ Devise a game in which the children identify a sound from an unseen source and decide whether it is a rattle, a bang, a bleep, a tap, a hum or a scrape.

◆ Encourage the children to search for things in the room that move with a push or a pull. They can use stickers to highlight these: one colour for things that are pushed, another for things that are pulled.

◆ Provide a collection of toys for the children to sort according to their own criteria. They might choose to group them according to shape or size, or whether or not they have wheels.

Further literacy ideas

◆ Point out the importance of labels for providing other people with information. Encourage the children to write their own labels and captions for the groups of objects.

◆ Underline the words spoken by Mum and point out the words used to describe how she speaks: *said, shouted, called, cried.* Refer to the exclamation marks and the question mark, and explain how this punctuation helps to indicate how the words are spoken. The children can practise reading the spoken words, using appropriate tones of voice, and join in a reading of the whole story.

◆ Help the children to collect words with the same spelling pattern as *toy*: *boy, joy, enjoy, destroy* and so on. Ask them to write a sentence using all these words.

◆ Help the children to find more words that begin with the same two letters as *pull* and *push* (such as *pullover, puppet, punch*). Ask them to invent and practise a tongue twister based on this sound.

◆ Ask the children to write a simple sentence that might be spoken by their parent or teacher, relating to an everyday activity. It could be a statement, command or question (with a full stop, exclamation mark or question mark respectively).

Genre
introduction

Introducing Flat Stanley (1)

Flat Stanley
Jeff Brown

Stanley Lambchop is just a normal healthy boy, though since a large notice-board fell on him, he's been only half an inch thick!
For Stanley this presents no problems, in fact he finds he can do all sorts of things and go to places never before possible.

Jeff Brown's hilarious text and Tomi Ungerer's equally funny drawings make this book absolutely irresistible.

Introducing Flat Stanley (2)

Genre
story

When Stanley got used to being flat, he enjoyed it.

He could go in and out of rooms, even when the door was closed, just by lying down and sliding through the crack at the bottom.

Mr and Mrs Lambchop said it was silly, but they were quite proud of him.

Arthur got jealous and tried to slide under a door, but he just banged his head.

Being flat could also be helpful, Stanley found.

He was taking a walk with Mrs Lambchop one afternoon when her favourite ring fell from her finger. The ring rolled across the pavement and down between the bars of a grating that covered a dark, deep shaft. Mrs Lambchop began to cry.

'I have an idea,' Stanley said.

He took the laces out of his shoes and an extra pair out of his pocket and tied them all together to make one long lace. Then he tied the end of that to the back of his belt and gave the other end to his mother.

'Lower me,' he said, 'and I will look for the ring.'

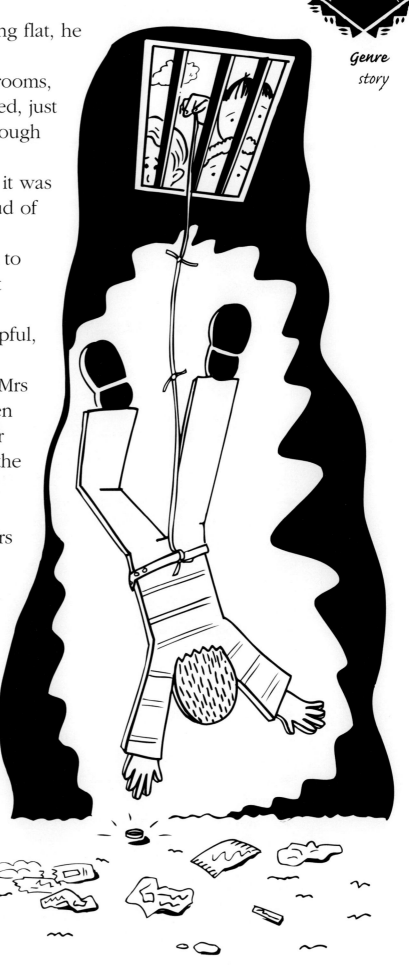

Introducing Flat Stanley

The introduction text (from the book cover) explains Stanley's current state, and the story text begins one of his adventures.

Arrange a part of the classroom to display a collection of things that are flat and thin (see 'Science activities').

Science learning objectives

◆ To use their senses to explore and recognize the similarities and differences between materials (Sc3 1a).

◆ To sort objects into groups on the basis of simple material properties (Sc3 1b).

◆ To recognize and name common types of material (Sc3 1c).

◆ To find out about the uses of a variety of materials and link these to their simple properties (Sc3 1d).

◆ To find out how the shapes of some materials can be changed by some processes, including squashing (Sc3 2a).

Discussing the text

◆ Explain that by describing Stanley as flat, the author also means that he is thin (like a sheet of paper). Ask the children to tell you what they know about things that are flat and thin. Look for examples around the room. Are some things flatter (thinner) than others?

◆ Talk about the introduction text which has been taken from the back cover of the book. Explain that this is known as the 'blurb', and is meant to be read before the book. Ask the children whether they think it is helpful to have a blurb. Perhaps it gives you an idea of what the story is about and helps you to decide whether you want to read it.

◆ The introduction tells us that Stanley is 'only half an inch thick'. Explain that this is just a bit bigger than a centimetre and ask the children to show you how big this measurement is with their fingers.

◆ Look at the classroom door and any other doors in the classroom. Could Stanley slide under any of these?

◆ Talk about the parents being proud and Arthur being jealous and what these feelings are like. Who do the children think Arthur might be? Do they have any experiences of brothers and sisters or themselves being proud or jealous?

◆ Besides slipping under doors and down grates, what else would the children like to do if they became flat?

◆ Discuss whether anyone could really be as flat as Stanley. Do the children think Jeff Brown, the author, knows Flat Stanley?

Vocabulary

Materials, wood, plastic, metal, paper, flat, bend, touch, pushing, pulling, squashing, changing.

Science activities

◆ Show the children a collection of things that are flat and thin: an envelope, a leaf, a biscuit, a ruler, plastic shapes, a baking tray, a mat, a piece of card, a sheet of newspaper, a tile and so on. Ask the children for ideas about how these items can be grouped. They may suggest sorting according to the type of material (paper, wood, plastic and metal), or into groups of things that can bend or be folded and things that cannot. The children can list and draw the six flattest (thinnest) things they know.

◆ Discuss 'flat' as meaning 'having a smooth or level surface' (as in a road, for example). Does the floor have a flat surface? The table? The door? Identify surfaces of materials that are not flat and smooth, such as fur, gravel or corrugated cardboard.

◆ Invent a game for identifying flat (thin) things by touch. The children can use blindfolds or feely bags to sort objects into those which are flat and those which are not.

◆ Discuss the uses of things that are flat (thin): encourage the children to think of putting things in piles, slotting things into small spaces, using a flat surface, packing things in boxes and so on.

◆ Give the children equal-sized lumps of Plasticine or play dough (one per child) and ask them to make flat shapes. Ask what actions they used to flatten the material (perhaps squashing, pressing or pushing). Are all the flat shapes the same size and thickness? Can the material be changed back to its original shape?

Further literacy ideas

◆ Focus on the words *hilarious* and *irresistible* in the blurb. Can the children suggest what each word might mean? What kind of story would the children expect *Flat Stanley* to be from this information.

◆ Discuss the words *flat, flatter* and *flattest*. With the children, compose three sentences that show how these words are used.

◆ Collect other 'fl' words, such as *flutter, flip, flop, fly* and *float*, and create a nonsense sentence that the children will enjoy speaking.

◆ Encourage the children to write the rest of Stanley's adventure, from where he goes through the bars of the grating. What would it be like down there? Would he be able to see properly? Would the children enjoy this experience? Does Stanley find the ring? How does he get out?

◆ The children might like to imagine themselves as flat and very thin, and write about an exciting adventure they might have. Alternatively, they could invent a flat friend for Stanley and write a collaborative class story describing what the two of them do.

◆ Write out the words 'as flat as a pancake'. Ask the children whether they think a pancake is really the flattest and thinnest thing they know. Could they improve on this saying? What would their new comparison be? They can write out their ideas for display.

The Snowman

Genre
rhyming
poem

Mother, while you were at the shops
and I was snoozing in my chair
I heard a tap at the window
saw a snowman standing there

He looked so cold and miserable
I almost could have cried
so I put the kettle on
and invited him inside

I made him a cup of cocoa
to warm the cockles of his nose
then he snuggled in front of the fire
for a cosy little doze

He lay there warm and smiling
softly counting sheep
I eavesdropped for a little while
then I too fell asleep

Seems he awoke and tiptoed out
exactly when I'm not too sure
it's a wonder you didn't see him
as you came in through the door

(oh, and by the way,
the kitten's made a puddle on the floor)

Roger McGough

The snowman

Display pictures of snow scenes. Ideally, this poem should be presented to the children on a cold, wintry day – with snow as a bonus.

This poem leads children to consider their experiences of melting snow.

Science learning objectives

◆ To explore and describe the way some everyday materials change when they are heated or cooled (Sc3 2b).

◆ To conduct an investigation: planning and predicting, testing, recording and trying to explain results (Sc1 2a–j).

◆ To recognize that there are are hazards in materials and physical processes, and assess risks and take action to reduce risks to themselves and others (Breadth of study 2b).

Discussing the text

◆ Help the children to appreciate the joke of this poem. What is Roger McGough trying to make us think as we read through the poem, and what has really happened?

◆ Bring to the children's attention the references to sleeping: *snoozing, doze, asleep, awoke*. Could the child in the poem have been dreaming about a snowman?

◆ Discuss some words and phrases that might puzzle the children. Do they know that counting sheep is supposed to be a way of sending yourself to sleep, and that eavesdropping means listening in to something not meant for you? Explain that people usually talk about 'warming the cockles of your heart' – but the child warms the cockles of the snowman's nose. Why is this? Could it be that the poet wants that line to rhyme with *doze*?

◆ Ask the children which words of the poem tell them that it was a warm and cosy room. They might suggest: *snuggled in front of the fire; warm and smiling; cup of cocoa*. Which contrasting words tell them what it was like outside?

Vocabulary

Hot, warm, cold, freezing, melt, boil, heat, heated, steam, materials, ice, snow, warmer, warmest, colder, coldest.

Science activities

◆ Encourage the children to compile two lists: one of things that are hot (using red and orange pens) and one of things that are cold (using blue and silver pens).

◆ Take this opportunity to warn the children of the dangers of very hot things, and discuss how they can avoid getting burned or scalded. Talk about open fires, cooking appliances, boiling kettles and hot water. Remind the children that very cold things can be dangerous too – for example, ice straight from the freezer can damage skin.

◆ Explore the effect of heat on different foods. Provide some hard-boiled egg, baked dough and cooked potato for the children to compare with the same materials in their unheated states. Ask the children whether the things that have been heated can be changed back to their original state. Ask them to consider

why we heat egg, dough and potato; explain that new materials have been made which are easier for us to digest.

◆ Explore the effect of heat on materials that are likely to melt. Put some chocolate, butter, candle wax and ice (an ice cube) in small foil dishes in a warm place – either above a hot radiator or floating in a container of hot water. Encourage the children to predict what will happen; perhaps they will suggest the order in which the materials will melt.

◆ When appropriate, allow the children to bring balls of snow inside the classroom to observe what happens. Do all the balls melt at the same rate? Perhaps the children can relate the snowballs' size and density (how closely packed they are) and the room's temperature to the melting process.

◆ Provide pairs with an ice cube in a plastic container. Challenge them to keep the ice from melting for as long as possible. Encourage them to plan a strategy beforehand, recording what they intend to do and making careful observations during the test. Make a block graph to record how long the ice cubes lasted, perhaps by filling in a square for every five minutes.

◆ Provide the children with appropriate vocabulary and help them to create a concept map relating to *hot* and *cold* (see illustration below.)

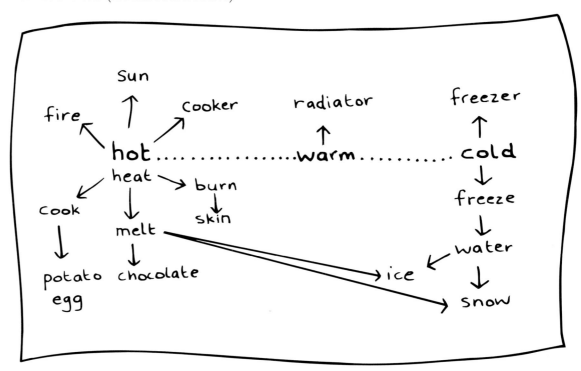

Further literacy ideas

◆ Ask the children to provide suitable words to describe being warm and cold: *As warm as...As cold as...*

◆ Present the words *cold, colder* and *coldest*. Ask the children to make up sentences to compare different cold things.

◆ Collect other words and phrases that could be used to build up a picture of being in a warm and cosy room, and others that could describe the cold winter outside. Display the children's suggestions, using appropriate pictures and colours to illustrate the contrast.

◆ Locate and highlight the rhymes in the poem. Find other words with the same rhymes.

◆ Ask the children whether they know of any other poems or stories about a snow person – and if so, who wrote them. You could refer to examples such as the stories by Raymond Briggs and Hans Christian Andersen. The children can write their own Snowperson Story.

Winter Morning

Genre
*non-rhyming
poem*

On cold winter mornings
When my breath makes me think
I'm a kettle,
Dad and me wrap up warm
In scarves and balaclavas,
Then we fill a paper bag
With bread and go and feed the ducks
In our local park.
The lake is usually quite frozen
So the ducks can't swim,
They skim across the ice instead,
Chasing the bits of bread
That we throw,
But when they try to peck the crumbs
The pieces slip and slide away.
Poor ducks!
They sometimes chase that bread
For ages and ages,
It makes me hungry just watching them,
So when Dad isn't looking
I pop some bread in my mouth and have a quick chew.
The ducks don't seem to mind,
At least they've never said anything
To me if they do.

Frank Flynn

Winter Morning

This poem reminds children of the changes that can take place in winter: how the cold affects both water and living things.

Read this poem in anticipation of a hard winter – or, more appropriately, during a cold spell. Display pictures of icy conditions, including those of arctic lands. Obtain a video of ducks, geese and swans, so that the children can observe their movements (especially on ice). Collect some different fabrics and items of winter clothing. Organize access to a freezer.

Science learning objectives

◆ To know that animals move, feed, grow and use their senses (Sc2 1b).

◆ To know that humans and other animals need food and water to stay alive (Sc2 2b).

◆ To find out about the uses of a variety of materials and how these are linked to their simple properties (Sc3 1d).

◆ To explore and describe the way some everyday materials change when they are heated or cooled (Sc3 2b).

◆ To recognize that there are hazards in materials and physical processes (Breadth of study 2b).

Discussing the text

◆ Talk about wrapping up warm on a winter's morning. What clothes do the children find are the warmest? Do any of them wear a balaclava?

◆ Find out whether all the children like ducks. What is it that makes ducks so appealing? Talk about the children's experiences of feeding ducks. Are there any in their local park? Have they ever fed ducks in winter?

◆ What does Frank Flynn mean when he writes 'my breath makes me think / I'm a kettle'? Unless there have been some really frosty mornings, the children might not have experience of this.

◆ Has it been cold enough for ponds to freeze over this winter? The children might not yet have real experience of a severe frost. Encourage them to anticipate a spell of really cold weather by commenting regularly on the 'feel' of a morning: is there a frosty feel in the air; or is it springlike?

◆ Ask the children what excuse the child in the poem gives for eating the ducks' bread. Does he really need an excuse?

Vocabulary

Change, water, ice, melt, melting, warm, warmer, freeze, materials, move, movement, danger.

Science activities

◆ Provide the children with a collection of fabrics to explore. They should use their sense of touch to sort the fabrics into those that feel warm and will be useful for winter clothes, and those that feel suitable for summer wear. If blindfolds or feely bags are used, the influence of colour and pattern will not obscure the scientific test. Attach small pieces of each fabric to a chart, on which the children can record the reasons for their choices.

◆ Use a video of ducks to demonstrate their movements. Ask the children how ducks get from one place to another. Do they know that ducks can walk, swim and fly? What other birds can do these three things?

◆ Find out what the children know about water turning to ice and ice turning to water. How do we make water turn to ice in the home? Fill a variety of containers, such as plastic tubs, bags and balloons, with water and leave them in a freezer for a few days.

◆ Provide each group with a deep tray containing the ice shape formed by a balloon. Let them observe the ice through one day in the classroom. Encourage them to observe and record its shape and texture, and any patterns they can see. What do they notice during the day? What changes take place? Why is the ice melting? Emphasize the cycle of water becoming colder, turning to ice, becoming warmer and melting to water again. Encourage the children to draw a diagram with arrows to show these processes.

◆ Ask the children which other materials might change from a liquid to a solid when put in a freezer. They might suggest orange drink, tea, soup, gravy, custard and so on. Use small amounts of these to test their predictions.

◆ Identify words in the text that describe how ducks and other things move on ice: *skim, slip* and *slide*. Compare these with the usual movements of a duck in water. The children can draw a duck and surround it with words relating to its movements in water, on ice, on land and in the air.

◆ Take this opportunity to warn the children of the dangers of frozen ponds and other stretches of water: however strong they think the ice might be, they should **never** venture onto the surface or allow a dog to walk on it. Explain that people have drowned trying to rescue pets that have strayed onto a frozen pond and then become trapped.

Further literacy ideas

◆ Collect names of winter clothes and make a dictionary of these. Look closely at the word *balaclava* and the pattern of letters it contains. Which words (such as *balaclava* and *anorak*) might have come from another language?

◆ Highlight and list the words associated with movement in the poem, such as *swim, skim, throw, peck, slip, slide* and *chase*. Add other words that describe the behaviour of ducks, such as *preen, waddle, quack* and *shake* (their tails).

◆ Ask the children how this poem is different from others that they know. You might refer to 'The Snowman' by Roger McGough (page 104). Have they noticed that it does not rhyme?

◆ The children can write their own story or non-rhyming poem about their experiences of going out on a cold winter morning or feeding birds.

Recipes

Genre
instructions

Tasty chocolate crunchies

These chocolate crunchies are easy to make and taste delicious!

You will need:

a block of chocolate
cornflakes

a small bowl
a saucepan
two large spoons
paper cake cases

**ASK AN ADULT
TO POUR THE
HOT WATER.**

**ALWAYS
TAKE CARE
WHEN USING HOT
MATERIALS.**

What to do:
1. First wash your hands.
2. Collect together all the things you need.
3. Break the chocolate into small pieces and put them in the bowl.
4. Stand the bowl in the saucepan.
5. Ask the adult to pour hot water into the saucepan.
6. Stir carefully until the hot water has melted the chocolate.
7. Take the bowl out of the saucepan.
8. Stir spoonfuls of cornflakes into the melted chocolate.
9. Spoon the mixture into paper cake cases and leave it to set.
10. Wash the bowl and spoons and tidy up.

Arrange your crunchies on a plate. Pass them round at teatime!

Fruity jelly

Everyone will love this jelly at teatime.

You will need:

1 packet of jelly
1 can of fruit
280 ml (½ pint)
    of boiling water

a measuring jug
a saucepan
a large bowl
a small bowl
a large spoon
a can opener

**AN ADULT TO OPEN THE CAN
AND POUR THE BOILING WATER.**

BEWARE OF SHARP EDGES AND HOT MATERIALS.

What to do:
1. First wash your hands.
2. Collect together all the things you need.
3. Spoon the fruit from the can into the small bowl, but save the juice in the can.
4. Break the jelly into pieces and put them in the measuring jug.
5. Ask the adult to pour the boiling water onto the jelly.
6. Carefully stir the jelly with a spoon until it has all dissolved.
7. Add juice (and some cold water if necessary) until you have 550ml (1 pint) of liquid in the measuring jug.
8. When the liquid has cooled a little, stir in the fruit.
9. Pour the mixture into a large bowl and put it in the refrigerator to set.
10. Wash up and tidy everything away.

Enjoy your fruity jelly!

Recipes

These simple recipes encourage children to follow instructions and explore how heating and cooling changes materials.

Use either or both of these recipes to show the children that we are using scientific knowledge when we prepare food.

Science learning objectives

◆ To know that eating the right types and amounts of food help humans to keep healthy (Sc2 2c).

◆ To find out about the uses of a variety of materials and link these uses to their basic properties (Sc3 1d).

◆ To explore and describe the way some everyday materials (for example, water, chocolate) change when they are heated or cooled (Sc3 2b).

◆ To relate their understanding of science to familar domestic contexts (Breadth of study 1a).

◆ To recognize that there are hazards in materials and physical processes, and assess risks and take action to reduce risks to themselves and others (Breadth of study 2b).

Discussing the text

◆ Encourage the children to talk about the features of the text. Do they recognize it as a set of instructions? Do they understand what recipes are?

◆ What are the instructions helping us to do? Could the children make a cake or a jelly without any instructions? Why is it useful to have numbered points telling us what to do?

◆ Do the crunchies and the jelly appeal to the children? Which would they prefer to make and eat?

◆ Ask why it is useful to have a list of the things needed at the start of the instructions. Does it help us with shopping? Does it help us to find the right equipment before we start?

◆ Can the children say what foods would need to be on their shopping list in order for them to make the crunchies and the jelly?

◆ Discuss why an adult needs to be involved, and remind children of the dangers of things that are hot or sharp. Why do the children think the warnings are written in capital letters?

◆ Encourage the children to consider why both sets of instructions start and end with similar points. Remind them of the importance of washing their hands before touching food.

Vocabulary

Materials, change, heat, cool, water, hot, cold, steam, eat, healthy.

Science activities

◆ Carry out the first recipe. Observe what happens when chocolate is heated, and what happens when it cools again. Make sure the children understand that it is the same material, although its shape has changed.

◆ Carry out the second recipe. Observe the changes that take place when jelly is stirred into the hot water (dissolving), and notice how it sets again when cooled.

◆ Provide samples of potato, bread, egg white, cake mixture and clay before and after heating. Ask the children to describe the differences they see and to say why we heat food and clay. Do they think the heated materials can be changed back to their original state?

◆ Ask the children to predict what will happen when chocolate, cheese and ice are heated. Which do they think will melt first? Put pieces of these near a warm radiator or on a sunny windowsill. Prepare a chart for the children to record their observations and explanations. Ask them to consider: *How have the materials changed? Can they be returned to their original state? How could this be done?*

◆ Ask the children what happens to water when it is heated. Boil water in a kettle so that the children can safely observe the steam. Warn them that steam can damage skin and point out that an adult is required to help with hot water in the recipes. What do the children think happens to steam? Demonstrate how it changes back to water when it touches a cool surface.

◆ Help the children to draw concept diagrams (see illustration below) that show what changes happen when familiar materials are heated and cooled.

◆ Talk about why we need to eat food: it is necessary for growth in children and enables all of us to stay alive and be active. Remind the children of the need to eat a range of foods and to eat more of some types of food than others. Do the children think chocolate crunchies and fruit jelly are important foods or are they treats? Would it be a good idea to eat only these? Can they think of some important foods that we eat that do not need to be cooked?

◆ Let the children examine a selection of cooking utensils and group them according to what they are made of. Can they suggest why metal is good for pans and spoons? (It is strong and does not melt when we are cooking.) Find out whether the children associate pottery bowls with clay and point out how useful it is that the hardened clay does not become soft again when the bowls get hot. Also consider the usefulness of glass bowls.

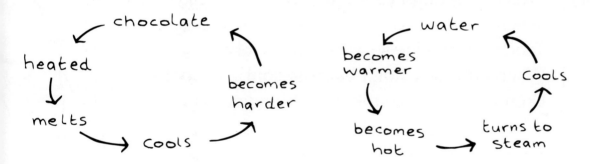

Further literacy ideas

◆ Provide a collection of utensils for the children to label, giving the name of each item and the material it is made from.

◆ Look more closely at the command words: *wash, collect, break* and so on. Help the children to recognize the style of language used for instructions. Do they think it sounds bossy? Does it save on words?

◆ Find the verbs *stir, pour* and *spoon*. Mime these movements. When do the children need to carry them out in their everyday lives?

◆ When the children have taken part in a different activity, such as planting a bulb, ask them to write simple instructions so that other people will know what to do.

◆ Encourage the children to rehearse the procedure for one of the recipes, using the correct utensils, so that they understand thoroughly what they will be doing during a cooking session.

◆ Focus on the initial letters of the foods involved (cornflakes, jelly, fruit). Make a food dictionary, trying to find examples for each letter of the alphabet.

Riddles: Materials

Genre
riddles

I am always very cold.
I fall from the clouds and cover the ground.
When it gets warmer I disappear.
What am I?

I am a very useful material.
I am strong,
But I can break into a hundred pieces.
You can see right through me.
What am I?

You cannot hold me in your hands,
I will slip through your fingers.
When I get very cold, I am hard and slippery,
Touch me and I will freeze your fingers.
When I get very hot, I become light and float away,
Do not try to catch me or I'll burn your fingers.
What am I?

Buckets, bowls, buttons and bottles,
Toys, trays and tiddlywinks.
Cups, counters, computers and coat-hangers,
Pens, packets and plates.
What can all these things be made of?

Riddles: Materials

Present the riddles one at a time, letting the children focus their attention on each.

These riddles introduce children to word puzzles, and encourage them to look for clues to the answers.

Science learning objectives

◆ To sort and recognize materials, knowing their properties and uses and that some are found naturally (Sc3 1a, b, c, d).

◆ To explore and describe the way some materials change when they are heated or cooled (Sc3 2b).

◆ To use simple scientific language to communicate ideas and to name and describe materials (Breadth of study 2a).

Discussing the text

◆ Choose an appropriate riddle to read - perhaps as an introduction to a science topic, in relation to current science work or as revision.

◆ Reveal the clues slowly, one at a time, giving the children plenty of time to think about each clue.

◆ Focus on the use of a question mark at the end of each riddle; point out that this means an answer is required. Encourage the children to give their answers as a simple sentence, rather than a single word.

◆ Point out that **all** the clues in each riddle must be considered to arrive at an answer.

Riddle 1

◆ Read the first line and ask the children to suggest things that are always very cold, perhaps making a list.

◆ After reading the second line, identify any of the suggestions that still fit the description.

◆ Decide whether the third clue confirms any of the children's ideas, and compose a sentence to answer the question (for example, 'You are snow').

Riddle 2

◆ After reading the first line, ask the children what materials they know that are very useful. Make a list of these.

◆ After revealing the next clue, identify which of the materials suggested are strong.

◆ The third clue should guide the children to the answer ('You are glass'), which will be confirmed by the next line.

Riddle 3

◆ Consider the first two lines of this riddle, giving the children time to think; but ask them to keep any ideas to themselves for the time being.

◆ Similarly, read the next pair of lines and then the final pair before asking the children what they think the answer to the puzzle might be.

◆ When the children have decided that the riddle is describing water and its other forms (ice and steam), ask them to explain the clues for each other's benefit.

Riddle 4

◆ Read the whole riddle, perhaps twice, before asking the children to suggest an answer. Discuss all ideas, valuing opinions and comments before finally deciding that each of the items could be made of plastic.

Vocabulary

Materials, useful, break, freeze, burn, question, answer, clue.

Science activities

Riddle 1

◆ If a convenient snowfall occurs, take the opportunity to observe and investigate snowflakes. Encourage the children to talk about the way the snowflakes move as they fall, what happens when they alight on different surfaces and how easily they melt.

◆ In the absence of snow, display pictures and show a video of snow scenes and magnified snowflakes.

Riddle 2

◆ List items that are made from glass. Explain that glass is a manufactured material, not a natural one. Talk about the properties of glass: it is transparent and strong; it can be made into thin sheets, as well as a variety of different shapes; glass objects can be attractive to look at. Discuss why glass is used for particular purposes.

◆ Point out the hazards associated with using glass: it can break into sharp, very dangerous pieces; people may walk into a transparent piece of glass, not realizing that it is there.

Riddle 3

◆ Give the children an opportunity to observe and investigate water turning to ice, either on a wintry day or using a freezer. Remind them that ice straight from the freezer should not be touched. Reverse the process and encourage the children to investigate the melting of ice.

◆ Taking the necessary precautions, heat water until it turns to steam. Show the children what happens when steam touches a cool surface. Point out that steam can cause burns to skin.

◆ Link the processes involved when water turns to ice and when it turns to steam. Help the children to build up a concept map using the words *changes, cools/cooling, heats/heated, water, ice, steam, boils/boiling, freezes/frozen*.

Riddle 4

◆ Make a collection of things made from plastic and ask the children to find ways of grouping them. Talk about the usefulness of plastic.

◆ Ask the children to identify items in the riddle that might be made of other materials: buttons from metal, toys from wood, packets from paper and so on.

◆ Explain that plastic is a manufactured material. Identify other manufactured materials such as glass, nylon and brick. Provide a collection of items for the children to sort according to whether they are natural or manufactured.

Further literacy ideas

Riddle 1

◆ Provide the children with words relating to temperature, such as *cold, very cold, cool, warm, hot* and *very hot*. Ask them to order these words, from the coldest to the hottest. Encourage them to think of other words to insert into their list.

◆ Ask the children to make sentences including comparisons such as *warm, warmer* and *warmest* or *cold, colder* and *coldest*.

Riddle 2

◆ Suggest that the children compose their own riddles to describe other familiar materials, such as wood, paper, clay, metal or plastic.

◆ Talk about how the word *useful* can be changed to mean the opposite: *useless*. Point out that the word *use* has the same meaning in both words.

Riddle 3

◆ Focus on the fingers as useful parts of the body. Ask the children to examine and draw their hands, and to consider the things their fingers help them to do. Make a class list of ten important things we need our fingers for during the day.

◆ Choose particular words to use for phonic or spelling practice.

Riddle 4

◆ Ask the children to substitute their own words for the names of items in the riddle (either keeping to the same initial letter or using any initial). Perhaps another line could be created, using words beginning with another letter of the alphabet. Sorting a collection of plastic items according to their initial letter might help with ideas for this.

◆ Make word collections of the names of metal and wooden items. Compose a riddle using these (not necessarily using repeated initial letters as in the original riddle).

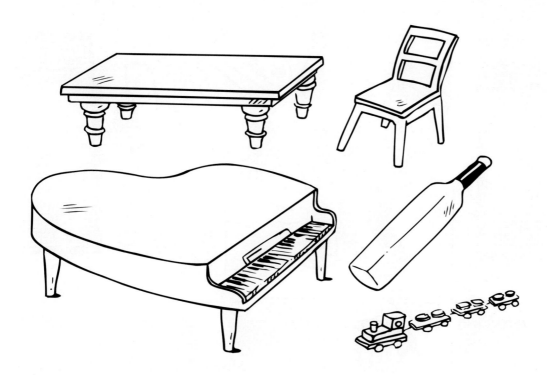

Physical processes

The texts in this chapter focus on the phenomena of electricity, movement, light and sound, and introduce children to the ways in which these physical processes affect our daily lives.

The children are reminded how dependent we are on electricity through being asked to identify the appliances we rely on during one day. The difference between mains electricity and electricity produced by a battery is highlighted, and emphasis is placed on the dangers of mains electricity and the safe methods of handling all electrical equipment.

Patterns of movement are explored through some of the texts, which explain how forces – especially the force of the wind – are involved in our everyday experiences.

Through the texts, the children are asked to use their senses to explore darkness, light and sound. At the same time, they are made aware of the hazards of bright lights – especially the Sun – and very loud sounds.

Wherever possible, the children are encouraged to explore and investigate physical processes: creating their own circuits, experimenting with a range of movements, relating the effects of the wind to their understanding of forces, experiencing degrees of darkness, and practising making loud and soft sounds.

Links can be made through some of the texts to other areas of science – for example, the effects of darkness and light can be related to the lives of humans and other animals.

Something we cannot do without

Genre
information

Electricity is useful.
We cannot do without it. But electricity is dangerous. We must always take care when using it.

Power stations make electricity all day and all night. The electricity travels along miles of wires to reach our homes.

We need electricity to power a light, so that we can see when it would otherwise be dark. We need electricity to power a heater, so that we are warm when the weather is cold. We can watch television, listen to the radio and use computers because of electricity.

The mains electricity supply, which runs to all our homes, is so powerful that it can kill people.

Sometimes we use batteries when we need electricity. Batteries are safe to hold. We can use a battery to provide electricity that will light a torch, make a toy work or sound a buzzer.

Electricity moves around a circuit. You can make a bulb light up in a circuit with two pieces of wire and a battery.

DO NOT TOUCH ELECTRIC SOCKETS. HOLD PLUGS CAREFULLY WITH DRY HANDS.

Something we cannot do without

The text emphasizes our dependence on electricity and warns children about the dangers of mains electricity.

Display pictures of electrical appliances, and provide electric torches and toys for the children to examine. Make equipment available for pairs of children to make a simple circuit.

Science teaching objectives

◆ To know about everyday appliances that use electricity (Sc4 1a).

◆ To know about simple series circuits involving batteries, wires and bulbs (Sc4 1b).

◆ To develop scientific understanding through familar domestic contexts, and look at the part science has played in the development of many useful things (Breadth of study 1a, b).

◆ To recognize that there are hazards in materials and physical processes, and assess risks and take action to reduce risks to themsleves and others (Breadth of study 2b).

Discussing the text

◆ Talk about the purpose of the text: it provides information about electricity, and warns us about its dangers. Ask the children whether there is anything they have learned from this information. Do they think the information is useful?

◆ Discuss whether it is true that we cannot do without electricity. Ask the children to consider the ways in which they are depending on electricity at this time. Have they experienced a power cut? What did they do? Imagine a day at school without electricity. How would that affect everyone? What uses of electricity would they not like to be without?

◆ Remind the children of the danger of mains electricity. Why do they think part of the text is written in capital letters?

◆ Ask the children to tell you about things that use a battery to provide a supply of electricity. Have they tried making a simple circuit?

Vocabulary

Electric, electricity, power, power station, mains, safe, dangerous, circuit, battery, wire, bulb, light, buzzer, plug, socket.

Science activities

◆ Make a list of all the ways that the children have used electricity since they got out of bed: for light, warmth, heating food, keeping food cool, entertainment, learning and so on. They can record their personal dependence on electricity for the day, using drawings and sentences. Prepare a chart for each child on which they can tick off the electrical devices they have used each day; include a light bulb, heater, toaster, washing machine, fridge, television and computer.

◆ Emphasize the dangers of mains electricity. Identify the electrical sockets in the classroom and explain that plugs must always be handled carefully with dry hands. Ask the children to write a warning notice to remind others of the dangers.

◆ Give the children an opportunity to examine torches and other devices that use a battery for their power supply. Make sure they realize that, as these things are not connected to the mains, they are safe to handle – however, the batteries themselves should be handled with care as they contain poisonous chemicals. Talk about the different types of batteries available, and explain that the right battery is needed for each device. Identify the + and − symbols, and point out that the batteries must be correctly positioned for a device to work. Warn that very small batteries, such as those used in watches, could be swallowed and must be kept away from small children.

◆ The children can draw and label a device that uses a battery and talk about how the electricity is used in that device.

◆ Provide pairs of children with pieces of wire, a battery and a bulb, and ask them to make a circuit to light the bulb. They should draw and label their circuit, using their own symbols.

◆ With the children, create a diagram with arrows that demonstrates the journey electricity makes from the power station to a school and a home, and on to individual appliances.

Further literacy ideas

◆ Display a list of vocabulary for use in the activities listed below: *electricity, wire, battery, bulb, circuit, light, plug, socket.*

◆ Ask the children to create a poster warning people about the dangers of mains electricity.

◆ The children can write labels for a display of devices that use a battery; for the equipment needed to construct a circuit; or for identifying things that use mains electricity.

◆ Talk about opposites and the meanings of the words *light* and *dark, safe* and *dangerous, warm* and *cold.* The children can write sentences, with illustrations, relating these words to the uses of electricity.

Genre
story

Christmas lights

George's Gran gave him a tiny Christmas tree to decorate. His Mum and Dad were setting up the big tree by the front door. The first things to go on the big tree were the lights. Twenty-four different coloured bulbs along a green plastic rope.

'When we switch on, the mains electricity reaches each bulb along metal wire,' explained Dad. 'This green plastic material covers the wire to make it safe for us to handle.'

Mum said, 'We can put the plug in the socket now and switch on.'

They all counted together. 'Ten, nine, eight, seven, six, five, four, three, two, one, SWITCH ON!'

The lights shimmered and glowed.

'I would like my tree to have lights,' said George.

Mum found some wire, a battery and a few small bulbs. 'These are safe for you to handle. See if you can put together a circuit and make your own lights.'

George used sticky tape to fix the wires to the battery and a bulb. The bulb shone brightly.

'I could put this at the top of my tree for a star,' he thought.

Then George tried using two more bulbs in his circuit, so that he could make a string of lights.

'Three bulbs are not as bright as one bulb,' he told himself. 'I think I would rather have one bright bulb than three dim ones.'

George found some card. With scissors, crayons, glitter and glue, he created a brilliant star. He carefully made a hole in the middle of the star so that he could push the bulb through. When he connected the circuit again, it worked perfectly.

'Everyone come and see my magnificent tree,' he shouted.

Christmas lights

This story highlights the difference in power between mains electricity and the electricity produced by a small battery.

Collect equipment for making circuits: bulbs, equivalent batteries, wires, bulb holders.

Science learning objectives

◆ To know about everyday appliances that use electricity (Sc4 1a).

◆ To know about simple series circuits involving batteries, wires and bulbs (Sc4 1b).

◆ To know how a switch can be used to break a circuit (Sc4 1c).

Discussing the text

◆ Ask the children whether they help to decorate their houses at Christmas, Diwali, or other special occasions. Talk about the lights used on trees and around the home. Where does the electricity come from to make the lights work? Encourage the children to remind each other of the dangers of mains electricity and how they can keep themselves safe.

◆ Ask the children whether they have made a circuit. If so, did they do it by themselves or with help?

◆ What could George have used his lighted bulb for instead of a star? What would the children have used it for?

Vocabulary

Electricity, light, bulb, battery, wire, circuit, mains, switch, safe, dangerous, plug, socket.

Science activities

◆ Show the children the equipment required to make a circuit; identify each piece and discuss why it is needed. Explain that a bulb holder is not actually a part of the circuit but it makes things easier by keeping the bulb upright.

◆ Ask the children, working in pairs, to create their own circuit to light a bulb. They should draw and label the circuit. How could they use the lit bulb decoratively?

◆ Draw examples of circuits: some complete, others incomplete. (See illustration below.) Ask the children to predict whether each circuit will light a bulb and give reasons. Challenge them to build the circuits and change the incomplete ones so that they will work. Ask them to use their knowledge of circuits to explain what they have done.

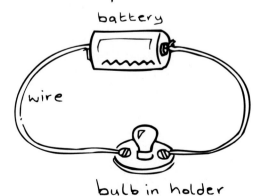

Complete circuit

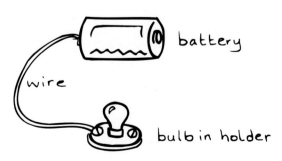

Incomplete circuit

Further literacy ideas

◆ The children can make a picture dictionary of the words relating to their work on electricity.

◆ Encourage the children to make an instruction sheet for others who might need to make a circuit. Remind them to start by listing all the equipment that is needed.

◆ The children can each write the numbers one to ten (in words) on small cards, then draw numbers of objects on other cards, then devise and play a matching game in pairs.

◆ Underline the words spoken by Mum, Dad and George in different colours. Encourage individual children to take over the reading of the conversation while you act as narrator.

◆ Make a collection of the words in the text that describe effects produced by light: *shimmered, glowed, shone, bright, brilliant.* Add any other words the children can think of.

The Windmill

Genre
shape poem

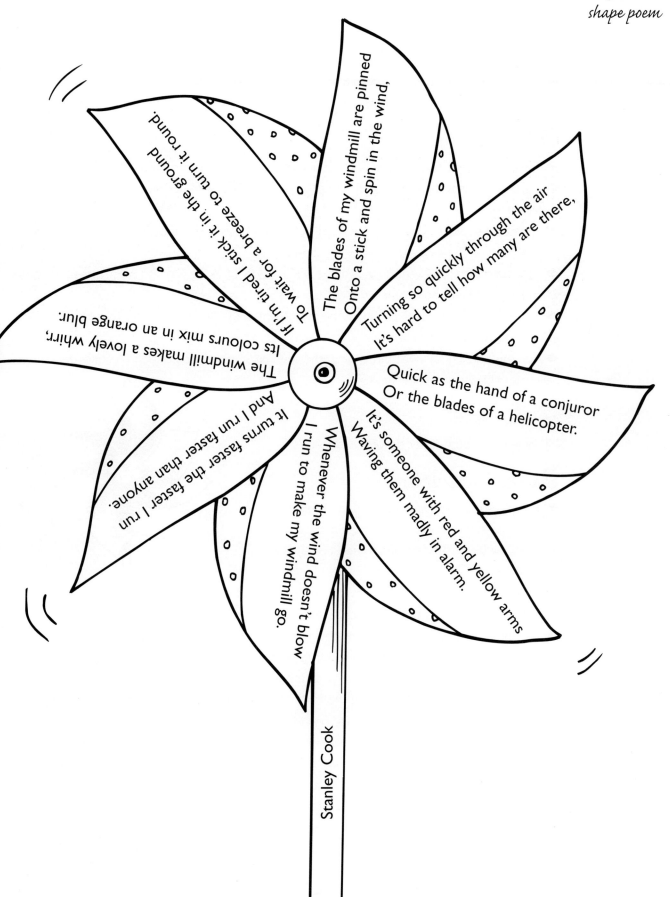

The blades of my windmill are pinned
Onto a stick and spin in the wind,

Turning so quickly through the air
It's hard to tell how many are there,

Quick as the hand of a conjuror
Or the blades of a helicopter.

It's someone with red and yellow arms
Waving them madly in alarm.

Whenever the wind doesn't blow
I run to make my windmill go.

It turns faster the faster I run
And I run faster than anyone.

The windmill makes a lovely whirr,
Its colours mix in an orange blur.

If I'm tired I stick it in the ground
To wait for a breeze to turn it round.

Stanley Cook

The Windmill

This poem shares with children the experience of playing with a toy windmill.

Obtain some multicoloured plastic or paper toy windmills for the children to explore.

Science learning objectives

◆ To find out about and describe the movement of familiar things (Sc4 2a).

◆ To know that both pushes and pulls are examples of forces (Sc4 2b).

◆ To recognize that when things speed up, slow down or change direction, there is a cause (Sc4 2c).

Discussing the text

◆ Confirm that this text is a poem. What kind of poem is it? Talk about how the words have been arranged on the drawing, and relate this to a toy windmill if possible. Tell the children that this is called a shape poem.

◆ Count the number of blades the windmill has and consider how this has determined the length of the poem.

◆ Talk about the colours and sounds of the windmill. How can the windmill be described as orange when the blades are red and yellow? What sort of sound is a 'whirr'?

◆ What does Stanley Cook say about the movement of the windmill? Identify relevant words: *spin, quick, quickly, waving, turns, turning.*

◆ Can the children say what three things the windmill reminds the poet of? (A conjuror's hands, a helicopter's blades, someone waving.)

Vocabulary

Movement, pull, push, faster, slower, wind, force.

Science activities

◆ Provide some toy windmills for the children to observe. Ask them to examine the shape of the blades. See how the blades are fastened to the stick, and how they turn.

◆ Encourage the children to provide descriptions of the windmill's movement, using words such as 'turn', 'spin', 'go round' and 'faster'.

◆ Ask the children what they do with their hands to make the blades start turning. Confirm that they use a push. Remind them that when they do this, they are using a force. Talk about how they could also use their breath as a force to push the windmill round.

◆ Take the windmills outside, so that the force of the wind can be seen to make them spin. Find a spot where the windmills go faster and a spot where they turn more slowly. Explain that the force of the wind is sometimes strong, sometimes more gentle, depending on the spot and the weather. Do the children think the force of the wind is greater than that of their breath? Do they realize that if this is so, the wind will make the windmills turn faster? Ask some children to run with the windmills while the rest observe. Discuss and record their observations.

◆ Put several windmills in the ground where they can be observed throughout the day. Compare the movement of windmills in different positions and at different times of the day. Encourage the children to record their observations and give their reasons for the differences in movement (for example, wind direction and amount of shelter).

◆ Compare a push with a pull. Can the children think of ways to make things move by pulling them?

◆ Give the children an opportunity to mix red and yellow paint during an art session. Compare this with the effect of the red and yellow blades 'mixing' their colours.

Further literacy ideas

◆ Identify the rhymes in the poem. Write them out as pairs and encourage the children to repeat them aloud, emphasizing the rhyme.

◆ Add to the collection of words describing the movement of windmills. Display these for the children to refer to as they write.

◆ The children can write sentences to record their experiences with toy windmills, describing the colours, sounds and movements.

◆ Provide other suitable shapes for the children to use as a framework and inspiration for writing poetry, prose or separate words – perhaps a flowerhead, a wheel or a star shape.

◆ Talk about using the words *fast, faster, fastest* and *slow, slower, slowest*. Ask the children to make up sentences using these words.

Flat Stanley flies

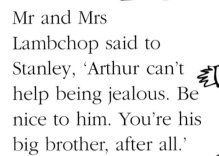

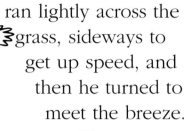

Mr and Mrs Lambchop said to Stanley, 'Arthur can't help being jealous. Be nice to him. You're his big brother, after all.'

Stanley and Arthur were in the park. The day was sunny, but windy too, and many older boys were flying beautiful, enormous kites with long tails, made in all the colours of the rainbow.

Arthur sighed. 'Some day,' he said, 'I will have a big kite and I will win a kite-flying contest and be famous like everyone else. *Nobody* knows who I am these days.'

Stanley remembered what his parents had said. He went to a boy whose kite was broken and borrowed a large spool of string.

'You can fly me, Arthur,' he said. 'Come on.'

He attached the string to himself and gave Arthur the spool to hold. He

ran lightly across the grass, sideways to get up speed, and then he turned to meet the breeze.

Up, up, up... UP! went Stanley, being a kite.

He knew just how to manage on the gusts of wind. He faced full into the wind if he wanted to rise, and let it take him from behind when he wanted speed. He had only to turn his thin edge to the wind, carefully, a little at a time, so that it did not hold him, and then he would slip gracefully down towards the earth again.

Arthur let out all the string and Stanley soared high above the trees, a beautiful sight in his pale sweater and bright brown trousers, against the pale-blue sky.

Everyone in the park stood still to watch.

Flat Stanley flies

Display some pictures of kites, as well as real (commercial) kites. Provide a home-made kite with a traditional tail to show the children when you are reading the text.

This story follows the one on page 101. It describes how Stanley can fly because of his flatness.

Science learning objectives

◆ To find out about the uses of a variety of materials and relate these to their simple properties (Sc3 1d).

◆ To find out about and describe the movement of familiar things (Sc4 2a).

◆ To know that both pushes and pulls are examples of forces (Sc4 2b).

◆ To recognize that when things speed up, slow down or change direction, there is a cause (Sc4 2c).

Discussing the text

◆ Talk about kite flying and the type of weather that is best for this activity.

◆ Remind the children that Arthur is jealous of his brother's flat shape, and discuss how Stanley tries to be nice to him. What do they understand by 'big brother'? Are any of the children big brothers or sisters? Do any of them have big brothers or sisters?

◆ Why do the children think Arthur wants to be famous? Would they like to become famous? What would they like to do that would make them famous?

◆ 'Arthur sighed.' Can the children tell you what a sigh is? They can practise sighing, and suggest times when they might want to sigh. Do they ever cause their parents or teacher to sigh?

Vocabulary

Move, movement, push, pull, force, speed, faster, slower, further.

Science activities

◆ Identify the words in the text that describe movement, such as *flying, ran, rise, slip, turned, soared.* Establish what kind of movement each word describes. Encourage the children to help you make a list of movements that a kite would make, including *twist, twirl, float, dive, spin, swerve* and *swoop.* If possible, show a video of kite-flying.

◆ During a PE session, ask the children to try movements such as twisting, spinning, turning and gliding. Also ask them to move forwards, backwards and sideways, both as a wide, spread out shape and as a narrow, closed in shape.

◆ Remind the children of words used to compare movements, such as *go faster, go slower* and *go further.* Ask them how they would make a wheeled toy go faster, slower or further.

◆ Explain that pushes and pulls are both **forces** that can cause or stop movement and ask the children to demonstrate examples of each in the classroom (such as pushing or pulling a door, pushing a book across a table, pulling a cap onto a head).

◆ Talk about the wind pushing a kite and making it fly. Ask the children what other things they have seen the wind pushing. They should mention litter and leaves blowing about, washing on the line, trees bending and swaying, windmills turning and themselves as they try to walk along. They can create a windy day picture.

◆ Discuss the best materials for making a kite. Describe the properties the materials need if they are going to be pushed by the wind: light in weight, flat, strong.

Further literacy ideas

◆ Make a list of any unfamiliar words with their meanings – such as *jealous, contest, famous, spool, edge, soared* and *breeze*.

◆ Ask the children how they can identify those words in the text that are spoken by Arthur, Stanley and their parents. Point out the speech marks, and highlight each person's spoken words in a different colour.

◆ Ask the children to write a description of a kite they would like to have: its colour, shape, pattern and tail. Then ask them to draw their kites on a separate sheet. Display the descriptions and drawings, so that the children can match words with pictures.

◆ Encourage the children to write the next part of the story. What might happen when Arthur got tired of kite flying? What if he let go of the string?

◆ Talk about the colours of the rainbow. Try to create a rainbow sculpture by arranging items and pictures of different colours in a band across a flat surface. Label each colour band, focusing on six colours: violet (or purple), blue, green, yellow, orange, red.

◆ Talk about words with the same ending as *kite*, such as *white, bite, polite* and *quite*.

The Owl Who Was Afraid of the Dark (1)

Genre
contents

CONTENTS

Genre
story

The Owl Who Was Afraid of the Dark (2)

Plop took a deep breath. 'The small boy said DARK IS EXCITING. The old lady said DARK IS KIND. The Boy Scout said DARK IS FUN. The little girl said DARK IS NECESSARY. The Father Christmas Lady said DARK IS FASCINATING. The man with the telescope said DARK IS WONDERFUL and Orion the black cat says DARK IS BEAUTIFUL.'

'And what do you think, Plop?'

Plop looked up at his mother with twinkling eyes. 'I think,' he said. 'I think – DARK IS SUPER! But Sssh! Daddy's coming. Don't say anything.'

Mr Barn Owl came in with a great flapping of wings. He dropped something at Plop's feet.

Plop swallowed it in one gulp. 'That was nice,' he said. 'What was it?'

'A vole.'

*(from **The Owl Who Was Afraid of the Dark** by Jill Tomlinson)*

The Owl Who Was Afraid of the Dark

The contents page of this book indicates how dark is described in each chapter. The extract from the story summarizes how Plop, a young owl, has overcome his fear of the dark.

Display pictures of, and books about, owls (especially barn owls) and other nocturnal animals.

Science learning objectives

◆ To know about the senses that enable animals to be aware of the world around them (Sc2 2g).

◆ To find out about the different kinds of animals in the local environment (Sc2 5a).

◆ To identify different light sources, including the Sun (Sc4 3a).

◆ To know that darkness is the absence of light (Sc4 3b).

Discussing the text

◆ Discuss what a book contains, and how the contents page at the start can help us find out what is in the different chapters. Help the children to understand the layout of this contents page: the numbers 1 to 7 are the chapters, and the page numbers tell us where each chapter starts.

◆ Explain that the story is about a young owl called Plop who realizes he is afraid of the dark – which is a problem when you are meant to spend your days sleeping and the nights exploring your environment. Are the children sometimes afraid of the dark? Point out that most people are a little bit frightened in the dark if they are in a strange situation and cannot easily find their way around.

◆ Talk about the characters mentioned and their opinions of the dark. How do the children think darkness could be exciting, kind, fun, necessary, fascinating, wonderful and beautiful? (In the story, the small boy thinks dark is exciting because he can hide; people cannot see the old lady's wrinkles; the Boy Scout enjoys camping; the little girl realizes that we need to sleep; the Father Christmas Lady notices that things look different in the dark; the man with the telescope can see the stars at night; and the cat believes many things look better in the dark.)

◆ Talk about the children's reaction to the last part of the text. If necessary, explain that a vole is a small furry creature similar to a mouse, and that owls prefer their food alive and whole.

Vocabulary

Light, dark, darkness, senses, sight, see, eyes, hearing.

Science activities

◆ Ask the children what sources of light they can think of. Make a list of these; include streetlamps, light bulbs, decorative lights, warning lights, candles, fires, the Sun, the Moon and stars. Compare the brightness and colours of different light sources.

◆ Emphasize that we need light to be able to see things; the Sun enables us to see during the day, but at night we need other light sources. Create a dark area of the room, perhaps by covering a table with a large dark cloth or arranging drapes across a corner of the room. Arrange pictures and objects in the dark area for the children to explore using a torch. Warn the children that they must never look directly at the Sun, because it is so bright it will harm their eyes.

◆ Talk about how we recognize our surroundings because we see things with our eyes. Discuss which other senses we need to use when we cannot see so well because it is dark. Devise a situation where the children try to recognize each other and different objects in a darkened room. Can they use their sense of hearing to recognize people by their voices and musical instruments by their sound? Can they use their sense of touch to tell when they have reached a wall, or to select a particular item from a table?

◆ It is unlikely that the children will have experienced complete darkness. Ask them to suggest places where no light at all can reach (perhaps a deep cave or a cupboard with a tight-fitting door). In a darkened room, look for the spaces where light can still get through.

◆ Display pictures of owls, especially barn owls. Ask the children what they know about these birds, and how they are different from the birds that might visit their garden. (Barn owls are quite big, they have a hooked beak and sharp claws for catching their prey, and they hunt at night.) The children can create their own information sheet about owls.

◆ Find out what other creatures prefer to move around at night – for example, foxes, bats, moths and badgers. Give each child two identical outline drawings of the school; ask the children to make one picture into a daytime scene and the other into a night-time scene. Talk about the changes that will happen to this familiar environment – in particular, which animals might appear during the day and which might appear when it is dark.

Further literacy ideas

◆ Draw pictures of the characters mentioned and write their descriptions of the dark in speech bubbles. The children can match each description with the speaker.

◆ Encourage the children to look on the classroom bookshelf, or in the library, and find other books with a contents page. Do books other than story books have a contents page?

◆ Help the children to choose one of the chapter headings; they can use this to write a story based on their own experiences of the dark.

Noisy (and Quiet) Places

Genre

nonsense poem

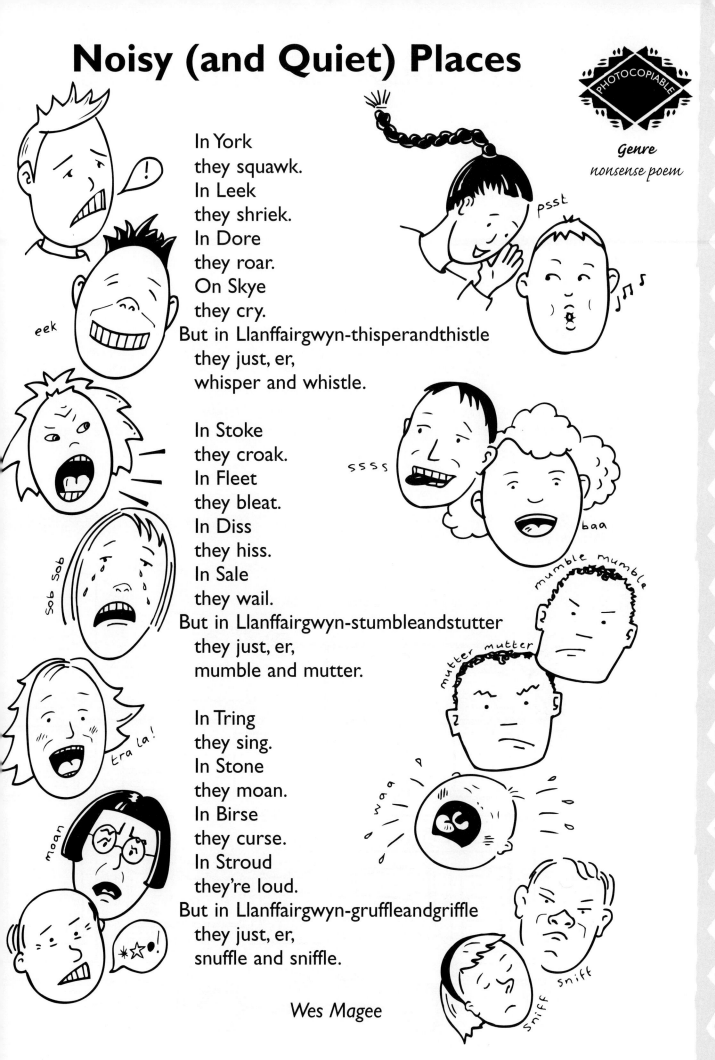

In York
they squawk.
In Leek
they shriek.
In Dore
they roar.
On Skye
they cry.
But in Llanffairgwyn-thisperandthistle
they just, er,
whisper and whistle.

In Stoke
they croak.
In Fleet
they bleat.
In Diss
they hiss.
In Sale
they wail.
But in Llanffairgwyn-stumbleandstutter
they just, er,
mumble and mutter.

In Tring
they sing.
In Stone
they moan.
In Birse
they curse.
In Stroud
they're loud.
But in Llanffairgwyn-gruffleandgriffle
they just, er,
snuffle and sniffle.

Wes Magee

Noisy (and Quiet) Places

Wes Magee uses place names and sounds to create a poem that is fun to read aloud.

Record some of the children's voices on tape for the class to identify.

Science learning objectives

◆ To know about the senses that enable humans and other animals to be aware of the world around them (Sc2 2g).

◆ To know that there are many kinds of sound and sources of sound (Sc4 3c).

◆ To know that sounds travel away from sources, getting fainter as they do so, and that they are heard when they enter the ear (Sc4 3d).

Discussing the text

◆ The children will need to hear this poem read to them more than once before they are ready to talk about it. Then ask them what sounds they heard and underline these in the text.

◆ Have the children heard of any of these place names? Perhaps one of the places is nearby. Ask how they can tell which words in the poem are place names. Do they know that these words begin with a capital letter? Do they think the three 'Llanffairgwyn...' places are real like the others?

◆ Decide which are the noisy places and which are the quiet places. As you read the poem again, ask the children to stand up for the noisy places and sit down for the quiet places.

◆ If appropriate, compare this poem with 'Surrounded by Noise!' (page 138). Which of these poems do the children enjoy more?

Vocabulary

Sound, loud, louder, quiet, quieter, further, away, nearer, noise, noisy.

PHYSICAL PROCESSES

Science activities

◆ Ask the children to sort the sounds of the poem into two groups: the loud and the soft. Encourage them to add other sounds that are not made by their voices, such as *bang, clap, clink* and *tap*.

◆ Ask the children to make different sounds with their voices, feeling their throats and faces as they do so and discovering the parts that move.

◆ Ask the children to close their eyes for a few minutes and listen to the sounds around them. Then ask them what they heard, and make a list. Can they recognize all the sounds, or are some from an unknown source? Try listening in another part of the school, or outside, and comparing the sounds.

◆ Ask the children to identify some recorded voices. Alternatively, devise a situation where they try to recognize each other's voices from behind a screen.

◆ Discuss the idea of 'high' and 'low' pitch. Produce a range of sounds for the children to group according to whether they think each sound is high or low.

Further literacy ideas

◆ Make sure the children are aware that each place name has been chosen to rhyme with a sound, then share the reading of the poem. As you read each place name line, they can follow with the rhyming line. Have they noticed that all the names, apart from the 'Llanfair...' ones, are short?

◆ Practise saying the words that end each verse: *whisper and whistle, mumble and mutter, snuffle and sniffle*. Make a collection of any other words the children know that begin in the same way as each of these pairs.

◆ Can the children think of any local place names that could be substituted for those in the poem? Perhaps they could make their own rhymes about places they know, using other 'sound' verbs.

Surrounded by Noise!

Genre
poem with
sound effects

I'm surrounded by noise,
LISTEN!

BEEP! BEEP! BEEP!
A car down on the street.
BOOGIE! BOOGIE! BOOGIE!
A disco beat.

THUMP! THUMP! THUMP!
A hammer next door.
THUD! THUD! THUD!
Brother jumping on the floor.

CLACKETY! CLACKETY!
CLACKETY!
A train rattles by.
ROAR! ROAR! ROAR!
A plane climbs the sky.

DRILL! DRILL! DRILL!
A workman on the road.
NO! NO! NO!
Mum about to explode.

We're surrounded by noise,
Just... STOP!
Just... LISTEN!

Ian Souter

Surrounded by Noise!

This poem emphasizes the level of noise that affects our everyday lives.

This poem should be read loudly.

Science learning objectives

◆ To know about the senses that enable humans and other animals to be aware of the world around them (Sc2 2g).

◆ To know that there are many kinds of sound and sources of sound (Sc4 3c).

◆ To know that sounds travel away from sources, getting fainter as they do so, and that they are heard when they enter the ear (Sc4 3d).

◆ To recognize that there are hazards in physical processes, and assess risks and take action to reduce risks to themselves and others (Breadth of study 2b).

Discussing the text

◆ Ask what makes this poem a 'noisy' poem. The children should mention the way it was read, the words that were used, the repetition and the scenes that are described.

◆ Are the sounds pleasant or unpleasant? Which of the sounds would the children least like to be near? What do we tend to do when we are close to very loud sounds? Where is the noisiest place the children know?

◆ Discuss why it is useful to hear such sounds, even though we might not like them. Talk about the warnings that sounds can give us when dangerous things are close by, such as cars or power tools.

◆ If appropriate, compare this poem with 'Noisy (and Quiet) Places' (page 135). Which poem do he children enjoy more?

Vocabulary

Noise, noisy, quiet, quieter, sound, hear, listen, further, away, loud, louder.

Science activities

◆ List the sources of sound mentioned in the poem and encourage the children to add other things that can make very loud sounds. Make a contasting list of sources of soft, quiet sounds. Are these all pleasant sounds?

◆ Use an alarm clock or percussion instrument to make a loud sound and ask the children what they can do to reduce the noise they are hearing. They might suggest covering their ears, moving away from the source of the sound or moving the source to another room. Ask them to draw diagrams with arrows to show the sound travelling from its source to their ears, with captions to show when the sound is loud and when it is soft.

◆ Ask the children to listen with their eyes closed. Make sounds from different parts of the room, and ask the children to point to where they think each sound coming from. Now ask them to try with one ear covered. Explain that we rely on comparing the information from both ears to identify the direction of a sound.

◆ Warn the children of the dangers of loud sounds, including loud music, too close to their ears: such sounds can damage the sensitive hearing mechanisms inside the ear. Talk about people such as tractor drivers and machine operators who need to wear ear protection.

◆ Out of doors, use a ringing alarm clock to demonstrate that sounds get fainter the further they are from our ears. Ask two children to walk away slowly with the clock while the others listen and describe how the sound fades. Does the sound reach a point when it cannot be heard at all? Does the sound change for the children who are walking with the clock?

◆ Still out of doors, encourage the children to listen very carefully for a few minutes and see whether they can identify any distant sounds. Can they identify the direction of each sound?

◆ Talk about sounds that warn us of dangers which we may be unable to see. Remind the children about listening for traffic when they cross a road, shouting a warning to others, hearing the sound of a reversing vehicle and so on. Discuss the idea of shouting or banging when help is needed and people's attention cannot be attracted in any other way.

Further literacy ideas

◆ Look at the way that Ian Souter has emphasized the noisy sounds by using capital letters, repeating words and using exclamation marks.

◆ Encourage the children to perform the poem with appropriate sound effects.

◆ Ask the children to create a new pair of lines for the poem, using another noisy sound and naming its source. Put these together to make a new poem, which will not need to rhyme.

◆ The children can write about their favourite sounds or the sounds they dislike the most.

◆ Write a class story together that can be recorded or performed with sound effects.

Riddles: Physical processes

PHOTOCOPIABLE

Genre
riddles

I am very far away.
I give the Earth light.
I make plants grow.
What am I?

There is something in this room you cannot see.
Something you must not touch.
Something you cannot do without.
It powers lights, the television and the computer.
What is it?

Sails turn,
Leaves flutter,
Flags wave,
Washing blows,
My hat flies away.
What makes all these things move?

I am in the box until you lift the lid.
I am in the cupboard until you open the door.
I am under a stone until you pick it up.
I am everywhere until the Sun appears.
What am I?

Riddles: Physical processes

These riddles introduce children to word puzzles, and encourage them to look for clues to the answers.

Present the riddles one at a time, letting the children focus their attention on each.

Science learning objectives

◆ To know about physical processes: appliances that use electricity; the movement of familiar things; light sources, including the Sun; darkness as the absence of light (Sc4 1a, 2a, 3a, b).

◆ To use simple scientific language to communicate ideas and to name and describe phenomena and processes (Breadth of study 2a).

Discussing the text

◆ Choose a riddle to read to the children - perhaps as an introduction to a science topic, in relation to current science work or as revision.

◆ Reveal the clues slowly, one line at a time, so that the children have plenty of time to think about each clue.

◆ Focus on the use of a question mark at the end of each riddle; point out that this means an answer is required. Encourage the children to provide a sentence for each answer, rather than a single word.

◆ Point out that **all** the clues in each riddle must be considered to arrive at an answer.

Riddle 1

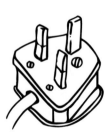

◆ Ask the children to close their eyes while you read each line slowly. Ask them to think about each clue, but to keep any ideas to themselves for the time being. At the end of the riddle, they should try to decide on an answer. Read the riddle again, asking the children to check their answer mentally with each clue.

◆ Ask for suggestions and check each answer against the clues, then read the riddle once more so that the children can reply together: 'You are the Sun'.

Riddle 2

◆ After reading the first line, give the children time to wonder what the clue is referring to.

◆ Read the second line and ask the children to suggest why it might be that they must not touch something. Accept all appropriate answers.

◆ After the next clue, elicit the children's thoughts about what might have have such a strange mixture of characteristics.

◆ The last clue will confirm that the riddle is describing electricity.

Riddle 3

◆ After a reading of this riddle, the children should suggest that the wind causes the movements described.

◆ Read the riddle again, encouraging the children to join in; they could perform suitable movements of their own.

Riddle 4

◆ Ask the children to close their eyes and listen to the clues. Read each line slowly while the children focus their attention on the clue.

◆ Ask for responses; help the children to interpret the clues and understand that darkness is being described.

Vocabulary

Light, grow, power, electricity, force, move, darkness, question, answer, clue.

Science activities

Riddle 1

◆ Emphasize that the Sun is the only source of light for the Earth. Ask the children where they think the Sun is at this moment.

◆ Warn the children never to look at the Sun directly; explain that its power can burn the eyes and cause blindness. Take this opportunity to advise them against exposing unprotected skin to strong sunlight.

◆ In the playground, ask the children to identify the position of the Sun by pointing towards it (without looking at it directly). On a cloudy day, ask the children where they think the Sun is. Emphasize that on the days when the Sun is not visible, it is obscured by clouds; but it is still overhead, bringing light and heat to the Earth every day.

◆ Make a list of the benefits of the Sun's light to living things.

Riddle 2

◆ Talk about the usefulness of electricity, and how difficult our lives would be without it. Make a list of appliances that need electricity to power them. Ask the children to draw pictures of the appliances they have used during one day; remind them that some of these, such as the fridge or the central heating, may be left on all the time.

◆ Warn the children of the dangers of mains electricity. Ask them to explain to each other the correct and safe use of electrical appliances.

Riddle 3

◆ Highlight the words in the riddle that describe movements. Can the children think of other movements associated with the wind?

◆ On a windy day, give the children an opportunity to experience the force of the wind and relate movements of objects to pushes and pulls. As the wind pushes, we have to pull to keep some of our clothes and belongings from being blown away by the wind.

Riddle 4

◆ Ask the children to identify the darker areas in the classroom. Discuss why these are darker than other areas. Make a list of places that the Sun cannot reach and which are therefore very dark.

◆ the children to help you create a really dark area, large enough for a child to experience. difficulties of keeping any place completely hidden from the Sun or any other light source, an get through.

Further literacy ideas

Riddle 1

◆ Ask the children to extend the riddle by composing other short clues that describe the Sun.

◆ Ask the children to make up clues for riddles about the Earth and the Moon.

Riddle 2

◆ Ask the children to write riddles about different things in the room. Display these around the room for other children to solve. The solutions can be drawn as pictures, to be matched with the appropriate riddles.

◆ Focus on the words in the riddle that have double vowels: *room* and *see*. Ask the children to suggest other words with the same sounds.

Riddle 3

◆ The children can extend the riddle with other movements caused by the wind.

◆ They can describe various movements in short sentences, perhaps constructing a sequence – for example: 'Bell rings. Door opens. Children walk in. Door closes.'

Riddle 4

◆ Talk about the opposite words to the verbs in the riddle, such as: *lift* and *drop*; *open* and *close*, *pick up* and *put down*, *appear* and *disappear*. Can the children tell you what the opposite of *everywhere* might be?

◆ Encourage the children to compose their own 'I am' riddle, describing anything they choose.